THE NORSE
DISCOVERY
OF AMERICA

Paul H. Chapman

One
Candle   Atlanta, Georgia U.S.A.
Press

Also by this author:

The Man Who Led Columbus to America

(Assessments may be found in Appendix C.)

Copyright 1981   One Candle Press
Library of Congress Catalog Card Number: 80–82715

ISBN 0–914032–02–X
Manufactured in the United States of America

Dedicated to

Dr. Warren L. Cook, *Professor of History, Castleton State College, Vermont;*

Dr. Cyclone Covey, *Professor of History, Wake Forest University, Winston-Salem, N.C.;*

And the other individuals in the academic world who have had the courage to be truth seekers when their findings did not fit the popular concept.

Contents

List of Charts and Maps

Pictures and Illustrations

Foreword

When I was trying to get my first book published, one of the Ivy League editors took some pains to write a friendly rejection letter. I had to know the reason why and picked up the telephone.

He talked freely. (His name is being withheld here to avoid any embarrassment to him for the words to follow). He compared *The Man Who Led Columbus to America* to Immanuel Velikovsky's *Worlds in Collision,* the publication of which had been stifled by the academic community. And he predicted I would never get it published by a university press. "It is too far from previously accepted concepts."

He was 90% right. Of the 44 University Presses in America to whom an outline was submitted, 40 were not willing to consider reading the manuscript; only four were and of those the one to whom it was sent did approve it for publication. (See editor James Travis's statement in Appendix C.)

I could appreciate what the Ivy League Press editor was saying, as I had been brash enough to state that the popular theory of historians as regards Columbus coming up with the idea that the world was round, was just not so; that an earlier person, Brendan, had visited America and discovered the Trade Wind Route in so doing; and that Columbus had used this information to accomplish his voyage, without which it would have been impossible.

In 1979, my publisher considering a second edition, sought to correct any errors of fact in the book which may have been discovered within the intervening six years. Awards were offered, and notices sent to the history departments of American universities and colleges. It was set up in such a manner that if only one error was found the claimant would be paid $1,000. There were 195 pages of facts in the text and notes of *The Man Who Led Columbus to America*—leading to different conclusions from the textbooks they were teaching. But there was not a single claim.

Now, after doing a navigational study of the Vinland voyages, I will be brash enough to claim to have found Vinland—which scholars have been seeking for a century and a half; to have located each of the three lands and seven specific locales visited by Eric's sons, daughter and son-in-law; to offer evidence in five fields of study as regards the continuing Norse immigration prior to our Colonial period; and cite the significance this had both for the later explorers and for us today.

I challenge you.

Paul H. Chapman

Acknowledgments

First and foremost I wish to publicly thank my co-worker on the research for this book as well as my co-worker in life, my wife Fran.

Magnus Magnusson (the author of the *Vinland Sagas* along with co-author Hermann Palsson), kindly granted permission to quote their translations of the Sagas. Their book, in addition to the translations, contains a broad coverage of the historical data associated with the Vinland Sagas. Magnusson, born in Iceland, a former Rector of the University of Edinburg, is a celebrated author and translater in early Norse subjects. His latest endeavor is the television series "Vikings!" on which he is the narrator. In the U.S., this appears on PBS, The Public Broadcasting System, in England, on BBC, The British Broadcasting Corporation.

The librarians at Emory University Library in Atlanta, the Library of the Maritime Museum in Newport News, Virginia, the Library of Congress, Washington, D.C., the Library in the Nova Scotia Archives in Halifax, the Newfoundland Public Library's Board in St. John's, as well as my local libraries, The Atlanta Public Library and the Chamblee unit of the Dekalb County Library System. All have been most helpful. Thank you.

Individually I wish to thank Donal B. Buchanan, who translated the words on the Spirit Pond Mapstone; Margot Maria De Chatelaine, Executive Director of the Society of Inter-Celtic Arts and Culture, for numerous contacts and introductions to Celtic specialists; to James C. Kelly of the Language Department of the Canadian Coast Guard College for background information on both languages and the Cape Breton local history; to Doug Maginley, navigation instructor at the Coast Guard College, for his counsel on navigational matters as well as his playing the role of "devil's advocate" in my meeting with him (one of our problems in this field is that we lack knowledgeable, constructive critics); to Samuel Skinner, Chief Officer on the Canadian National Ferry ship to Labrador, for pictures along that coast; Malcolm Pearson not only for his photographs of the Spirit Pond Stone used herein, but also for his briefing from his wide background of knowledge on this situation (Malcolm has done much of the photography work throughout New England dealing with the pre-Columbian subjects); to Baxter Pynn, lighthouse keeper at St. Anthony's in northernmost Newfoundland who took me around the hills in that area; and to Rex Boyd, the "bush pilot" who came in from his base at Main Brook in his seaplane (skis replace pontoons in the wintertime) in order to fly me around this area.

And finally those who have had the burden of wrestling with the barely legible notes, along with the barely intelligible voice tapes, my thanks go to my secretaries, Jacqueline Krizmanich and Mary Jo Shirer, for a job well done.

I

The Problem

If the Norse did indeed discover America, where did they land?

Today, there is general acceptance among historians and geographers that the Norse did discover and explore at least a part of America circa 1000 A.D., almost 500 years prior to Columbus. Ancient manuscripts, found in Iceland and called "Sagas," relate such events. But the question which has nagged historians is *where?*

The name given to the new land in the Sagas is "Vinland," sometimes called "Vinland the Good." As will be subsequently seen, the name continued in usage by the Scandinavian people right into the period of the Spanish discovery of America by Christopher Columbus, and beyond. Like other European colonies, Vinland was named peculiar to the European peoples who settled it; it was not the name the natives had applied to it and was obviously a name which changed as did the subsequent occupiers of the land. Canada was "New France" before the English won the French and Indians wars; New York was "New Amsterdam" before the English took it away from the Dutch, etc.

Those who have studied the Vinland location question have come up with remarkably different conclusions. These range all the way from Baffin Island, down past Newfoundland, the Gaspe Peninsula, Nova Scotia, Cape Cod, Rhode Island, to Virginia and the Carolinas. In other words, take any area on the eastern seaboard of North America and at least one study will have included this as the landing site of the Norse discoverers.

Why? One reason is the content of the Sagas which contained references to both "grapes" and to "no snow." To find wild grapes in America one has to come down into the New England states, and to find an area of no snow it would, under present conditions, be necessary for the location to be at least as far south as coastal Virginia, and more likely the Carolinas. Others have argued that there may have been dramatic changes in the climate affecting both the absence of snow and the presence of the grape.

In 1964, the *National Geographic* magazine published an article "Vinland Ruins Prove Vikings Found the New World."[1] A Norwegian explorer and writer, Helge Ingstad had spent years looking for Vinland. Now beside a bay on the northern tip of Newfoundland he felt assured, as he stated, he "had discovered the first proven remains of a Norse settlement in the Americas." The site, on most maps, is labeled L'Anse Aux Meadows.

Ingstad's article relates in a candid manner how his search had begun in Rhode Island and continued northward; that he had finally been directed to this particular site by local people living nearby. It is an isolated spot, so one wonders if other Norse sites in more isolated areas remain yet uncovered? Or in other areas, if Vinland might have been covered over by nature and/or by acts of man? After all, we still haven't found the original English Colony site of Jamestown; and this was constructed some six centuries closer to the present time.

The *National Geographic* article cites the verifications made by American archeologist Henry Collins of the Smithsonian Institute and Junius Bird of the American Museum of Natural History. But it must be noted that both simply confirmed this to be a Norse site and made no statement in regards to whether it was Vinland.

Subsequently, several of America's best known writers have included the L'Anse Aux Meadows site in their studies. Noted geographer Carl O. Sauer recognized Ingstad's ancient village, but with the additional parenthetical comment, "Ingstad admits Vinland is extending south from there." Sauer himself concludes the location of Vinland as being "southern New England, and preferably Long Island Sound, as indicated as the location of Vinland. There is no need of climatic change."[2]

C. W. Ceram, an archeologist whose books have been widely circulated, recognizes the Ingstad findings in his book *The First American*.[3] He says of the find "there no longer seems to be any doubt that the 'longhouse' had been Leif Erickson's house." In a paradox, Ceram next quotes Ingstad himself, who does not go that far, but simply says "to judge by all the material available to us, it is probable that the Norsemen who stayed at L'Anse Aux Meadows about a thousand years ago were identical with the Vinland voyages of the Icelandic Sagas." Furthermore, Ingstad in his book on the subject, *West to Vinland*,[4] makes this still further qualification in recognizing that the Sagas talk of two different sites which he now refers to as Northern Vinland and Southern Vinland. (These terms the Norse themselves did not use.)

Samuel Eliot Morison, America's prominent historian on the discovery period, states: "Finally, in 1960, a Norwegian archeologist named Helge Ingstad located a spot in northern Newfoundland, L'Anse Au Meadow, which he thought might be 'it.' Years of summertime diggings by competent archeologists have (it seems to me beyond reasonable doubt) proved this place to have indeed been Vinland. So, now that the location of Vinland has been solved, we may proceed . . ."[5]

In the same year that the *National Geographic* was publishing its account of Ingstad's findings here in America, another report on the same subject was being published in Norway by *Research in Norway*, sponsored by the Royal Ministry Foreign Affairs, a central committee for Norwegian research, and the Norwegian Research Council for Science and the Humanitist. It showed a considerably wider time range for occupation at the site.

The findings of the age (by Carbon 14 methods) of the various materials dug up at the L'Anse Aux Meadows' site and listed by the Canadian Museum located there are shown in the table reproduced here.

The *Viking Ship*, published by the Leif Erickson Society in the United States, reprinted the table from *Research in Norway* along with the comment "The results seem to be disastrous for the Ingstad theory that *this* was Vinland . . .

CARBON 14 DATES FROM L'ANSE AUX MEADOWS

Site	Material Analyzed	Date AD
Charcoal Kiln	Charcoal	820±70
Smithy	Charcoal	1060±70
Smithy	Charcoal	860±90
Cookpit #2	Charcoal	810±90
Cookpit #1	Charcoal	780±90
House F	Turfwall	1000+50
House F	Whalebone	1025±100
House F	Charcoal	870±70
House F	Charcoal	700±70
Sauna	Charcoal	1080±70
House E	Charcoal	820±70
House D	Charcoal	900±70
House A	Charcoal	640±30
House A	Turfwall	1000±90
House B	Charcoal	740±110
House C	Charcoal	710±130

Note the many samples which appear to fall in the six to seven hundred AD range."

Magnus Magnusson in *Viking Expansion Westwards* also recognized the work of Ingstad and his wife Anne Stine Ingstad, who did much of the archeological diggings. But he says of the L'Anse Aux Meadows site, "If this was Vinland, then Vinland was a confidence trick."[6]

The *Annals of the Association of American Geographers* in 1969 published a review article "analyzing the opinions of many of the more prominent authors who had delved into the subject." Its conclusion: "There is not a Vinland; there are many Vinlands. Its disputed location on the Northeastern American coast is only one example of the disagreements and controversies which characterize Vinland scholarship during the last century and one half. The survey of the literature of this period on the subject of the Medieval Norse in America yields a maze of contradictory, personalized, irreconcilable opinions and conclusions."[7]

Having completed my navigational study before sitting down to write, I believe that I have reconciled the various questions raised and have found the true location of Vinland. A detailed explanation follows.

II

Tools for Solving the Problem

A problem for historians in understanding the Sagas is the understanding of the navigational information given therein. It is a problem which by training and experience I am equipped to handle having been a Ferry Command navigator during World War II.

As Will Rogers once said, "We are all ignorant—on different subjects."

The Air Force, Navy, and Coast Guard Academies all teach navigation but are not in the business of teaching historians. The liberal arts schools in this country, on the other hand, do not teach navigation, but do educate our historians.

I was recently struck by the lack of knowledge on the subject while attending a seminar on exploration in which archeologists, historians and at least one astronomer were in attendance.[8] The speaker, in the course of a comprehensive presentation, asked for help from the audience: Could anyone tell him how ancient peoples had been able to find North? Much to my surprise, no one other than I seemed to know the answer.

A navigator *must* know the answer to this. All directions are relative to North, this is the beginning point. The answer is not, as one might think, to simply look at the north star. Polaris, while presently very close to the celestial north pole, is not directly on it. And in years gone by it has been located at a considerable distance away from it. In fact so far away that other stars have been used as the "north star." How then did they find true north?

Just as they painted imaginary animals in the sky to identify star groupings, so they also had an imaginary man in the sky to locate true north, regardless of the location of the north star. Knowing that all of the heavenly bodies ro-

tated about the pole, they imagined the man's navel as being the celestial north pole. He stood upright with his two arms stretched outright from the elbow, with these four extremities thus forming the hour positions of 12, 3, 6, and 9 respectively in an imaginary clock. A navigator at sea, knowing the arc of the north star's circle about the pole, and its position at anytime, could interpolate the pole location.

This "man in the sky" is illustrated here.

This figure was also known as the "clock in the sky" because the ancients also inserted a line between each of the four extremity points and used the location of the north star as one would use the hour arm of a clock. The bearing of the north star to the celestial pole is done by the relative position of a nearby star or star grouping. Currently it is being done, as in this illustration, by the Little Dipper group. So it was in Columbus' time. Previously, in the time of the ancient Greek poet Homer, he referred to the Big Bear constellation as being the guide.

Studying the *National Geographic* article I was again struck by the lack of application of navigational knowledge to the subject. In a map depicting "The Westward Way of the Norsemen" they have shown the ocean currents involved in these areas, but have failed to show the prevailing wind pattern.[9] Winds account for about ten times as much of the movement as do currents, as applied to sailing ships in the North Atlantic. In some areas, such as in the Florida Straits where the Gulf Stream is constricted and has to flow at a rapid rate, it can be a larger factor than the air movement inasmuch as the trade winds here diminish.

But in the area of this study, the Davis Strait between Greenland and the mainland of North America, the currents flow northward on the east side and southward on the west

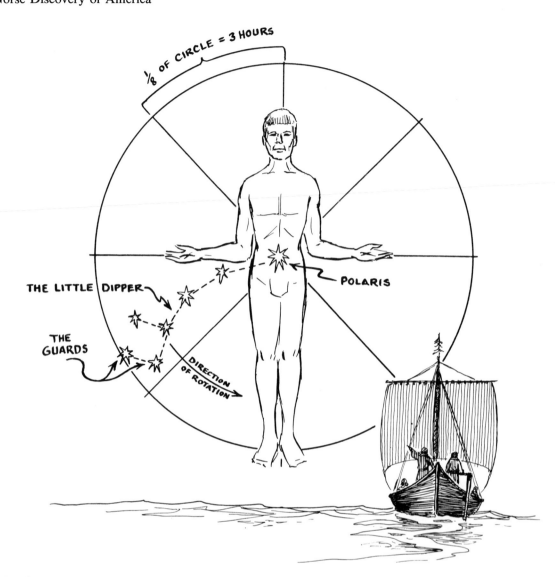

Clock In The Sky. Just as World War II fliers had an imaginary clock in the sky, so did the ancient mariners. During the war it served to locate attacking aircraft by giving directions relative to fore and aft of their own planes: the nose was "12 o'clock," an enemy squarely off the right side was at "3 o'clock" and one directly on the tail, "6 o'clock." The hours in between made location more precise.

The imaginary clock for early seamen centered on the North Star which was placed at the navel of an imaginary man standing with two arms outstretched from elbows at the body. A circle around him would be divided into 4 equal parts. Imaginary bisecting lines in each quadrant created 8 equal parts.

The "Little Dipper" group of stars, which are in a line leading directly off of the North Star, act as the hour arm of the clock, rotating (counter-clockwise to the observer) and making a complete circle every 24 hours—just as the sun does. Thus one-eighth of the circle would equal three hours.

side, thus largely offsetting each other. The net navigational effect is almost nil, as is shown on Chart 1. Nonetheless, this journal's map shows it as if it were the only effect and then proceeds to show Leif Ericksson's route as following this current, with a heavy red line. Nor is any mention made of the wind factor in the legend to the map.

Surely someone with navigational knowledge could do a better job of plotting the courses as related in the Sagas. The Sagas in a number of instances do give the courses and directions, and even speeds in terms of elapsed times (number of sailing days).

Several years ago I had tackled a similar subject, the question as to whether or not an Irishman named Brendan had reached America, with the source material being ancient manuscripts called *Navigatio Sancti Brendani,* (Saint Brendan the Navigator). Plotting each leg of the voyage directly from those manuscripts, and using our present day knowledge of the winds and currents of the North Atlantic as

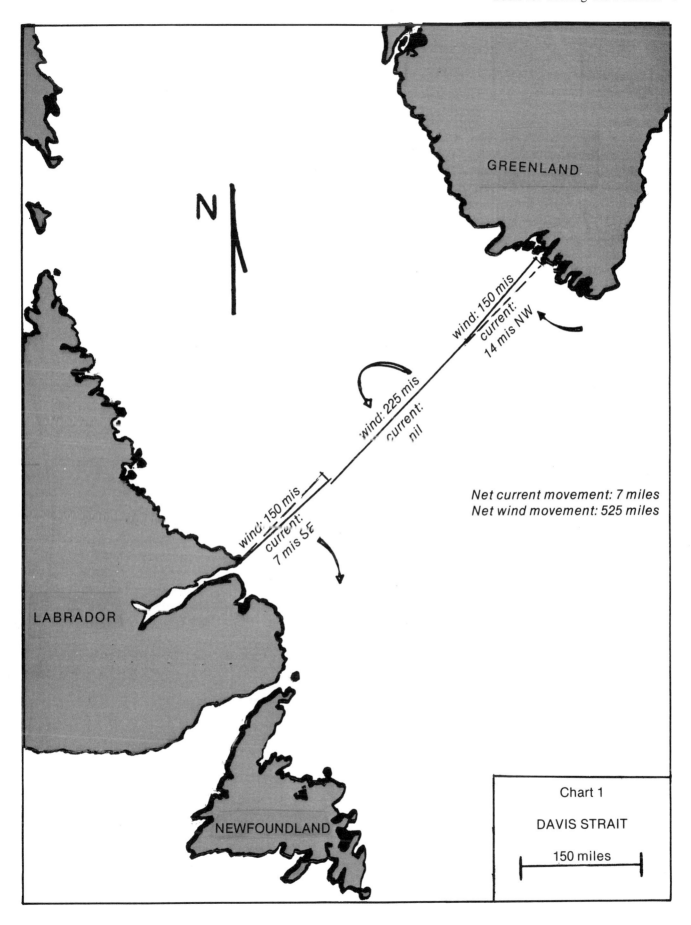

GREENLAND

N

wind: 150 mis
current:
14 mis NW

wind: 225 mis
current:
nil

wind: 150 mis
current:
7 mis SE

Net current movement: 7 miles
Net wind movement: 525 miles

LABRADOR

NEWFOUNDLAND

Chart 1

DAVIS STRAIT

150 miles

shown on the Pilots Charts, which in turn are published for each month of the year to accommodate the changing seasonal patterns, it was possible to retrace Brendan's journey to specific, identifiable locations. The geography of the landing sites confirmed the descriptions of the *Navigatio*.

This navigational study had won the plaudits of both sailors *(Sailing Magazine, Ensign)* and scholars *(The Library Journal, The New England Antiquities Research Association Journal)* as well as numerous individuals having expertise on various aspects of the subject. It was published in 1973 under the title *The Man Who Led Columbus to America.*[10] Assessments of this work can be found in Appendix C.

The original material with which we have to work on the Norse voyages is known as the "Vinland Sagas." These were found among the various Sagas which were located in Iceland at the time a decision was made to begin a collection and start a history of that nation, which was the parent of the Greenland and Vinland colonies.

Two of these Sagas deal with Vinland and they are respectively known as the Greenland Saga and Eric's Saga. The first one is believed to have been written down in the late 12th century and the second one not until the 13th century. There is also an earlier reference to the voyages written down by a neutral source, Adam of Bremen (Germany), about sixty years after the events had taken place, and corroborating these accounts.

The two Sagas concern the doings of only one family, that of Eric the Red and his children. As with all history it must be read in the light of the intent of the writer. The Sagas have all the earmarks of being the personal family histories written for the purpose of recording and glorifying the acts of ancestors, a practice which was popular among these people during that era. While the navigational information proves to be consistent (after all, these are just facts and figures), the recurring question of who is due credit for each accomplishment changes with the different versions.

The Greenland Saga credits an outsider to the family, Bjarni Herjolfsson, with first sighting lands to the west but makes the point of having Eric's son Leif land on them and name them. This narrative then devotes one chapter to each of the other three children of Eric, as well as a daughter and son-in-law, each of whom made voyages.

Eric's Saga, on the other hand, begins by citing Gudrid's (the daughter-in-law) ancestory. On becoming widowed from Eric's son, she married Thorfinn Karlsefni, who is then considered a son-in-law. This Saga has only a brief chapter on Eric's exploration of Greenland and then two more chapters on Gudrid and her background before coming to the fifth chapter which is described as "Leif Discovers Greenland." Bjarni is left out completely.

Next follows a chapter on the death of Eric's second son Thorstein, Gudrid's first husband. Now we come to a chapter on Karlsefni, her new husband to be, and this is followed by a chapter on the colonization voyage made by Gudrid and Karlsefni. It was on this trip that their first child Snorri was born. He is frequently cited as the first white child born in America.

The intervening voyage of Eric's third son, Thorvald, is garbled into the story and only briefly mentioned.

Eric's Saga winds up with a chapter on Karlsefni and Gudrid's descendants. It would appear that this second Saga should be called "The In-Law's Side of the Story." But while there are discrepancies, the substance of the two Sagas is the same. In a number of instances one provides navigational data which is omitted from the other, and therefore it is valuable to consider both.

But to do a comprehensive navigational study we need information about the Norse navigational abilities which is simply not found here. We need to know particularly ship speeds, the equipment they used, and their techniques of navigation. We are fortunate in having source material for all three of these needed areas of knowledge.

Norse ship sailing speeds. These are found in an Icelandic manuscript called the *Landnamabok* (Book of Settlements) which describes the settlement of Iceland during the period 870 to 930 A.D. It gives the sailing days (speed) between Norway and Iceland, between Iceland and Greenland, Iceland and Ireland, Iceland and Jan Mayen Island, and the direct route from Norway to Greenland. Since these encompass various prevailing wind patterns (head winds, side winds, and following winds) it gives us a schedule to apply to the varying wind conditions. The sailing ship, depending primarily upon wind for its movement, moves relative to the air speed and wind direction. Anyone who takes a shortcut and tries to use an overall average speed for all conditions is likely to reach the wrong location for the ships traveling range.

In addition, there is still another source on ship sailing speeds—Dicuil, the monk scholar in residence at the Court of Charlemagne who published his book on the *Measurements of the Earth.*[11] This has been combined with the *Landnamabok* and a study of this combined ship speed information is shown in Appendix A.

Time and distance are rather precise measurements. Therefore when the number of days sailing is stated and the ship's speed is known, the geographical range of the vessel can be ascertained. The Sagas give us the number of days sailing time between each of the lands found.

On the type of craft used, there is little question. The same basic single-masted, double-ended sailing vessel was in use in Europe throughout this period of history. Examples of it can still be seen today in the recovered vessels in the Viking Ship Museums both in Oslo, Norway and at Roskilde, Denmark. It is important however to understand both the ships' limits and capabilities.

Being "square rigged" it did not sail against the wind, as is done with today's "lateen rigged" sailing ships. It could

Square vs. Lateen Rig. The ship on the left is rigged with a square sail. It must have either a following wind or a side wind. It cannot move forward against a headwind. The ship on the right is rigged with a lateen sail. It can move forward with either a following wind or a headwind. The latter is accomplished through a zigzag pattern called "tacking."

The early Norse used the square rig pattern and thus were limited in their movements. Lateen rigging did not come into general use in Europe until centuries later.

Sketch by John Kollock.

only sail with a following or side wind. At other times it would have to wait for the wind pattern to change.

On the other hand it was a well-balanced craft, both fore and aft and across the beam. The high ends slashed through the waves in front, as well as dispersed the oncoming waves from behind during storms (when they had to run before the wind). It was a ship of shallow draft which in turn could go into shallow waters (something which Columbus's ships could not do and the cause of the loss of his flagship, the Santa Maria, while in the West Indies). It could be rowed as well as sailed (another feature lacking on the ships of later periods and one which caused Columbus to have to winter over on the unfriendly island of Jamaica during his third voyage).

It had such refined features as the folding mast which could be lowered during periods of freezing rain. Later "modern ships" were to suffer heavy losses due to ice build-ups on their superstructures causing capsizing. Deicing equipment, which was used on our aircraft during World War II, was later installed on these fishing boats.[12]

As to their navigational techniques, a single sentence from the *Landnamabok* tells a lot. It states "from Hern Island, off Norway, one can sail due West to Cape Farewell (Greenland's southern tip), passing north of Shetland close enough to see it clearly in good visability, and south of the Faeroes half-sunk below the horizon, at a day's sail south of Iceland." A navigator will note that the sailing directions are not from Bergen, the principal Norwegian seaport for the Greenland

trade,, but are from a small island to the North. Bergen is deep inland on a fjord, with an outlet to the sea at Hern. (Today, Hernar.) A line from Hern close enough to see the Shetlands, and then to see the Faeroes half sunk below the horizon are all on the same parallel within a half degree: 61 degrees north. This is also one day's sail south of Iceland as computed by the ships' speeds.[13]

So the first thing this sentence tells a navigator is that they were employing the "parallel sailing" technique. That is they sailed along a given parallel of latitude. To do this with precision it is necessary to have the type of navigational instrument which measures the sun and north star's angles above the horizon of the earth.[14] In modern times we call it a sextant. It has also been known as an octant and in ancient times more often as an astrolobe. The instruments have been constructed in different fashions, but the principle is always the same.

This single statement also gives us another piece of navigational knowhow: in directing the sailor to Cape Farewell, Greenland, which is at 60° N. latitude, they are sending him in one degree to the north or 60 nautical miles to the right of the intended target. This is known as the "landfall" technique. Navigation, while considered an exact science, is not so precise that there is not room for error. To avoid serious error, it was found that by making an intentional error on one side of a known line along a given target, the navigator could then turn in the known direction of the target and be assured of reaching it. Otherwise, if he

Norse Ship From Denmark. Here is a reconstruction, board-by-board, of a Norse ship. The original model was recovered from the channel nearby Roskilde, Denmark, and is in the Viking Ship Museum which is located there. The reconstruction was done by a group of boy scouts in cooperation with the museum.

This picture also illustrates the Norse ship's capability of moving forward with a side wind, and how it was accomplished: note how the sail is turned, and the wake of the ship.

Photo courtesy Vikingeskibshallen (Viking Ship Museum) Denmark.

misses his target he doesn't know where or when to turn. In this case, an error to the south could have thrown him hundreds of miles off course.

In addition to the astrolobe/sextant, the Norseman had a ships bearing dial, useful for obtaining direction from the sun. The dial itself has been found in archeological exploration work.

Still one more navigational tool is one which has only recently been re-discovered, the "sunstone." This is a mineral found in Norway and Iceland which has a peculiar property

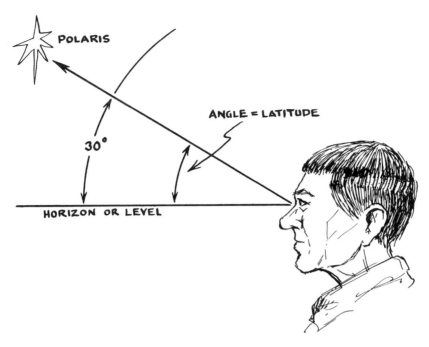

POLARIS

ANGLE = LATITUDE

30°

HORIZON OR LEVEL

Latitude By Polaris. Latitude has been possible to compute celestially since ancient times.

The sextant, and its earlier versions known as the "octant" and "astrolobes" go back into prehistory. The early Greeks reported the Phoenicians already had the instruments of navigation. This device measures the altitude of a star (planet, sun or moon) in a simple fashion: The bottom side of the angle is the line to the horizon, which can also be established in "plumb line" fashion with a perpendicular plane, the other side is another plane which rotates and is sighted much as an arrow would be. The amount of altitude is measured on a quarter circle by degrees—with a full circle divided into 360 degrees.

Latitude is calibrated in degrees, ranging from zero at the Equator to 90° at the earth's North Pole. Thus the range is the same as one quarter of a circle. When the north star (currently, Polaris) is level with the north celestial pole, then the latitude of the observer is the same as the altitude of the star.

In this example, the latitude of the observer is 30°N.

Both the time periods when the north star is level, and the arc for interpolating other times, can be ascertained from the clock in the sky, as shown on the first illustration.

Sketch by John Kollock.

of turning the sun's ultra-violet rays into visible light, thereby permitting the location of the sun even under a heavy cloud cover (Brendan the Irishman, became lost at sea when he was unable to find the sun or the stars under an overcast).

An eleven year old boy is responsible for our rediscovery of the sunstone. He is the son of Jorgen Jensen, chief navigator for Scandinavian Airlines, and having read the Norse Sagas he asked his dad if the sunstone might have a function similar to the suncompass used by Scandinavian pilots in flying over the North Pole (where the magnetic compass is valueless). Danish archeologist Thorkild Ramskou, who had been studying the problem for years, was told of the suggestion. He found that the minerals present along the western beaches could in fact locate the sun at anytime of the day, and in virtually any weather.

As with the St. Brendon's study, we have available to us the Pilots Charts of the North Atlantic showing the pre-

vailing wind speeds and directions as well as the currents flow. Each is shown for every five degree square of the ocean. Shown here is a section of the pilots chart for the area around Southern Greenland and the mainland of North America, the principal area of our study.

In modern historical times scholars have argued back and forth as to what land was found. But as we read the Sagas there is no doubt about the location among those Norsemen. They may have been uneducated but they knew how to follow the sailing information which had been given them. We should be able to do it also.

That which becomes readily apparent is that the Norse are now involved in not only a shorter course (as opposed to the previous courses between Norway and Iceland, Iceland and Greenland) but the winds along the course are also more favorable. Throughout the area of the North Atlantic there are prevailing westerlies—that is, winds blowing from the west. Headwinds to anyone crossing from Norway to

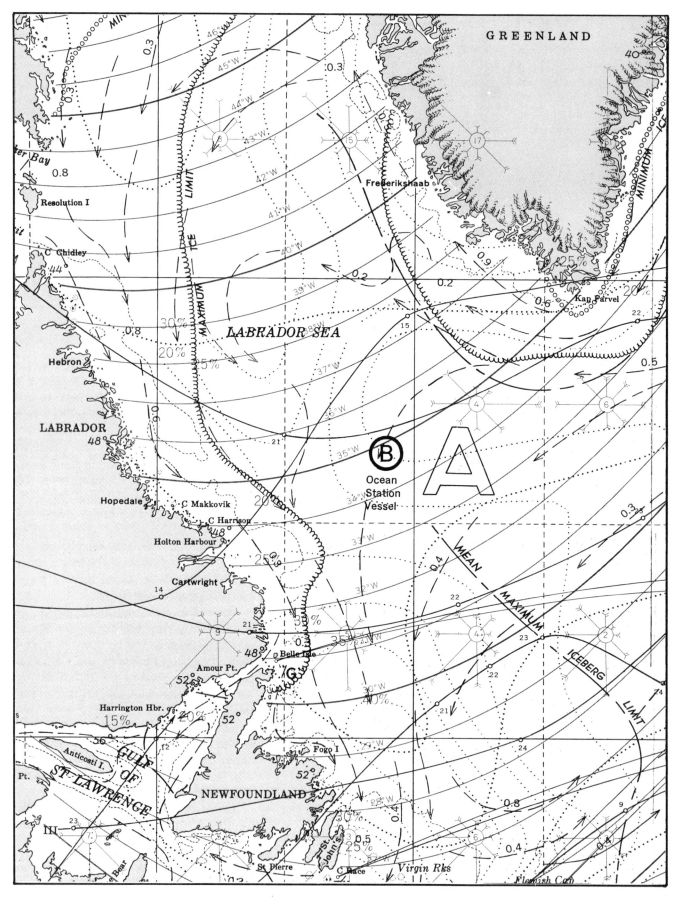

2. PILOT'S CHART
Area involved in the Vinland Sagas.
Dash lines show currents:
speeds are shown in knots
(nautical miles per hour.)

Iceland to Greenland. But now these same westerlies would become sidewinds on the north-south route between Greenland and Newfoundland. Useable winds.

Navigation, the kind which carried the early explorers back and forth across the North Atlantic as well as the kind which we used in ferrying airplanes across the same ocean during World War II, may be becoming a lost art. In the 1940's we flew into Newfoundland, Labrador, across Greenland, into Iceland, the Hebrides and Scotland—pretty much the same routes the Norse used. We landed at these places and could see the terrain—in fact we had to come to know it just as the Norse did, and for the same reasons, survival. But today the aircraft fly at jet plane speeds and

jet plane altitudes six and seven miles up in the air, and they fly directly from New York's airport to the European airport.

We depended primarily on celestial navigation, just as the earlier Norse had done. Nowadays planes fly across the Atlantic using various electronic devices, along with inertial guidance systems. All the pilot has to do is push a button and read a meter. Navigators are no longer required.

Can it be that this knowledge will be put aside and lost to future generations? One such example in which a whole field of knowledge has become lost because of lack of use also involves a facet of navigation: Portolan Charts are those early maps with many lines radiating outward from compass

Ferry Memorial, in the City of Gander, Newfoundland. Prior to World War II the only aircraft capable of flying across the Atlantic Ocean were literally flying boats—the old "clipper" planes. An exception was the occasional daredevil, the most famous and the first soloist being Charles A. Lindberg in 1927. During the war, with America becoming the "arsenal for democracy" it became necessary to develop aircraft and crews capable of making the crossing. One of the early models was the plane shown here, a medium bomber.

In order to get these short range planes across, it was necessary to shorten the distance by building an airfield in Newfoundland. Now, with additional gas tanks in their bomb bays, they could make it across.

Newfoundland made geographic sense for crossing the Atlantic by plane, just as it had earlier for the Norse who came by boat.

Photo by Frances H. Chapman.

Chart 3
TYPICAL PORTOLAN CHART

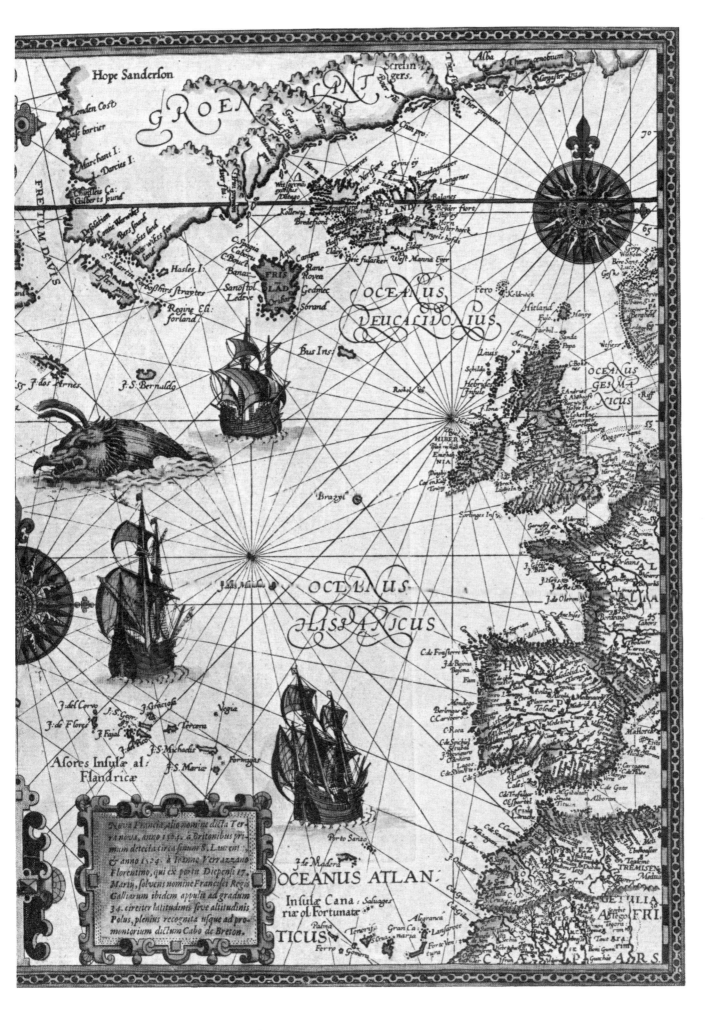

Hope Sanderſon

GROEN LANT

Screin gers.

Alba

Wit Monſter gotliche Dulago

ISLAND

OCEANUS DEUCALIDONIUS

Fero

Hitland

OCEANUS GERMANICUS

FRETUM DAVIS

Hasles I.

FRIS LAD

Regine Eli: forland

Bus Inſ.

Rockol

Hebride Inſulæ

HIBER Blak verketi Euerbati NIA

J.S. Bernaldo

Brazyl

OCEANUS HISPANICUS

Scrlinges Inſ.

J.del Cervo J.S. Geor: J.Graciosa J:de Flores J.Fajal Tercera J.S. Michaelis formigas J.S. Mariæ

Aſores Inſulæ al: Flandricæ

Vgia

C.de Finiſterre J:de Bayona Bayona Fam

HI A

Porto Santo

Nova Francia, alio nomine dicta Ter ra nova, anno 1504. à Britonibus pri mum detecta circa ſinum S. Laurenti & anno 1524. à Ioanne Verrazzano Florentino, qui ex portu Diepenſi 17. Martÿ, ſolvens nomine Franciſci Regis Galliarum ibidem appulit ad gradum 34. circiter latitudinis ſive altitudinis Polus, plenius recognita uſque ad pro montorium dictum Cabo de Breton.

J.de Madera

OCEANUS ATLAN TICUS

Inſulæ Cana: Saluages riæ ol. Fortunatæ

Palma Tenoriffa Gran Ca: naria Alegranca Lanſarote Fortu en tyra

Ferro Gomera

FEZ

GETULIA FRI.

A

roses, which seem to be randomly located. These are the antique maps frequently used in modern settings for decoration.

But in the time period before and after America's discoveries they had a different kind of purpose, a practical one. They were the navigator's—not the scholar's—maps. The term Portolan means "port finding." Their use ranged all the way north to Iceland, and south down to Portugal; then east and west across the width of the Mediterranean. They were in use right up into the 17th century, when the Mercator projection type of map won over acceptance because of the ease of direction plotting.

Yet in spite of its widespread use and the multitude of remaining examples, we cannot decipher the Portolan chart.

We do not know how it was constructed, nor how it was used. Our best modern cartographers cannot explain it.

We live in a day when our scientists can calculate the spherical trigonometry necessary to hit the "keyhole in the sky" and land a man on the moon, but we have lost the navigational knowledge of how to read the very chart used by most of the historical explorers and early colonists in reaching our own country.

While we still have a working knowledge of the other tools and techniques of the early navigators, this needs to be applied to the early records in order that we have a better understanding of the history of the discovery of America.

III

Courses

Bjarni Herjolfsson's Voyage

The Greenland Saga credits Bjarni Herjolfsson as being the first man to sight lands to the west of Greenland. Bjarni was an enterprising trader, spending his winters alternately at his father's home in Iceland, and abroad. On returning one year (either 985 or 986 A.D.), he found his father had sold the farm and left with Eric the Red to emigrate to Greenland.

As the Saga says

The news came as a shock to Bjarni and he refused to have his ship unloaded. His crew asked him what he had in mind; he replied that he intended to keep his custom of enjoying his father's hospitality over the winter—'so I want to sail my ship to Greenland, if you are willing to come with me.' They all replied that they would do what he thought best . . . They put to sea as soon as they were ready and sailed for three days until land was lost to sight below the horizon. Then the fair wind failed and northerly winds and fog set in, and for many days they had no idea what their course was. After that they saw the sun again and were able to get their bearings; they hoisted sail and after a day's sailing they sighted land.

"They discussed among themselves what country this might be. Bjarni said that he thought it could not be Greenland . . . (they decided to sail in close). Soon they could see that the country was not mountainous but was well wooded and with low hills. So they put to sea again, leaving the land on the port quarter . . ."

Bjarni had arrived in Iceland at Eyrar, a coastal village nearby the family farm. Departing from there in haste, they obviously did not await the more favorable winds as was considered good practice at the time (perhaps in their haste to make it to Greenland before the onset of the early winter).

Standing on a deck eight feet above sea level would have given them a visibility range of four miles, but the high land on the southwest corner of Iceland rising rapidly up to the 1,000-foot contour then gradually on up to 2,000 feet would extend the range of visibility to approximately fifty miles; add to this the fifty miles distance between Eyrar and lands end, and the distance finally made would be only some 100 miles in the three days voyaging. This is not unexpected inasmuch as westerly winds prevail. The slowness of their progress may have become a factor in their misjudging the distance covered on the next part of their voyage when the wind shifted. Obviously Bjarni did not have a sunstone as they "had no idea what their course was."

Greenland itself was still some 400–500 miles distance and they would have expected to approach it somewhat to the north along the east coast utilizing the "landfall" technique. This is the same approach which Eric himself had used earlier. However, as the text points out, as they entered the fog area the wind was coming in from the north. This blew them off course to the south and below the southern cape of Greenland; and as the text reads, they sailed "for many days" before sighting land. On sighting land, they found that it did not fit the physical description of Greenland which is an area of steep fjords and lofty glaciers.

On the lifting of the fog they stated "they saw the sun again and were able to get their bearings." The word "bearings" in plural is significant as there are two types of bearings which can be obtained from the sun: The azimuth bearing is the relative position of any body (a celestial body measured from its plumb line on the horizon) to the ship; the angle of the altitude to the celestial body is the other bearing. Taken at midday the sun is always due south and thereby north and all other points of the compass can be ascertained. An experienced navigator knows the sun's pathway for the respective time of year and can interpolate the azimuth bearing at other hours with a rough degree of accuracy. During nighttime, the polar star and its path relative to the north celestial pole (as explained earlier in Chapter II) also gives the bearing of north continuously thoughout the night. A noontime sighting of the sun on its celestial angle to the earth also gives an altitude bearing, which in turn reveals the latitude of the ship.

In this manner Bjarni and his crew knew that they had arrived on the east coast of a large land mass but recognized by the geographical descriptions that it was not Greenland. Having found that they were south of their objective they then turned north "leaving the land on the port quarter."

They continued this course and twice more closed in with the land, each time finding that it did not fit the physical description of Greenland. They knew they were too far south by the sun's and/or pole star's altitude bearings, and they must now have concluded that they had sailed too far west inasmuch as no such land had been reported east of Greenland. Now, as they near the latitude of Eric's settlement in Greenland they picked up a southwest wind, and they turned to the northeast "before the same fair wind" in order to continue to try and achieve the northerly latitude of the settlement, and at the same time backtracking eastward some of the distance that they had now found they had overshot. Had they still been at sea when the settlement's latitude had been reached, all they had to do was turn due east to reach it, this being another use of the landfall technique. But the manuscript does not mention this and instead reads in terms of direct contact being made on the same promontory where Bjarni's father's farm was located.

While Bjarni never landed on the mainland of North America, nonetheless his findings and his report were of such value that they continued to constitute the basic navigational information used by the other Norse people who followed. Charts #4-A and 4-B show Bjarni's courses. These have been ascertained by beginning at the end, which is a known location, and working backwards.

Here is how the Saga described it, in reverse sequence, and shown in italics. Navigational explanations follow each leg in regular type.

(A) *Once again they put the land astern and sailed out to sea before the same fair wind (from previous statement, southwest wind). But now it began to blow a gale and Bjarni ordered his men to shorten sail and not to go harder than the ship and rigging could stand. They sail now for four days until they sighted a fourth land . . . they made land as dusk was falling at a promontory which had a boat hull upon it. This was where Bjarni's father Herjolf lived and it has been called Herjolfsness ever since.*

We are here retracing Bjarni's voyage beginning with the last leg inasmuch as the final landing place is a known fixed

position. A northeast heading is indicated in the fact that they are sailing before the southwest wind. The gale force wind would move a ship at a maximum rate of speed in the range of 200 miles per day; however, that carries with it attendant risks to the ship and Bjarni, recognizing this, ordered his men to shorten the sail, and thereby slowed the ship's speed. The maximum ship speed as shown on the Norse time and distance tables is 150 miles per day (see Appendix A) and this is therefore used here as maximum safe speed. The fact that they were able to land before darkness set in indicates this should be counted as 3½ days sailing time. The east coast of Labrador lies in an arc across the Davis Strait from Greenland, at some 525 miles distance. The north bound current on one side of the Strait is offset by the south bound current on the other side making a negligible difference of 2.4 miles per day. Northern Labrador is the only land to lie in this direction from Herjolfness. Baffin Island lies to the northwest and would have required a southeasterly course; Newfoundland lies more to the South and a northeast heading from it would have bypassed Greenland.

(B) *They sighted a third land. This one was high and mountainous and topped by a glacier. Again they ask Bjarni if he wished to land there but he replied 'no, for this country seems to me to be worthless'. They did not lower sail this time but followed the coast line and saw that it was an island.*

The coast of Labrador north of Groswater Bay is a mountainous area ranging up to 5,320 feet. (The tallest mountain in North America east of the Rockies is Mt. Mitchell at 6,684 feet.) These mountains are sometimes on the coast and sometimes just off the coast sticking up as islands. The land is barren and can appropriately be described as "worthless." At the point towards the sea there are close in islands which because of the topography would have to be circled to ascertain they were islands.

(C) *. . . He ordered them to hoist sail and they did so. They turned the prow out to sea and sailed before a southwest wind for three days before they sighted a third land.*

Norse ships, while being square rigged, were capable of sailing with a side wind. We learn from the manuscript, and its progress in sequence, that they were sailing coastwise.

At the average side wind speed of 100 miles per day, for the three-day period they would have covered approximately 300 miles. Following the coast would necessitate some "in and out" maneuvering, reducing the net total distance covered. How much is a matter of judgement. My estimate is by a third, thus netting about 200 miles.

It is likely since they used the term "before they sighted" that they had crossed Groswater Bay, a wide opening between two land areas which gives the appearance from the sea of a separation into two separate lands. It is both wide

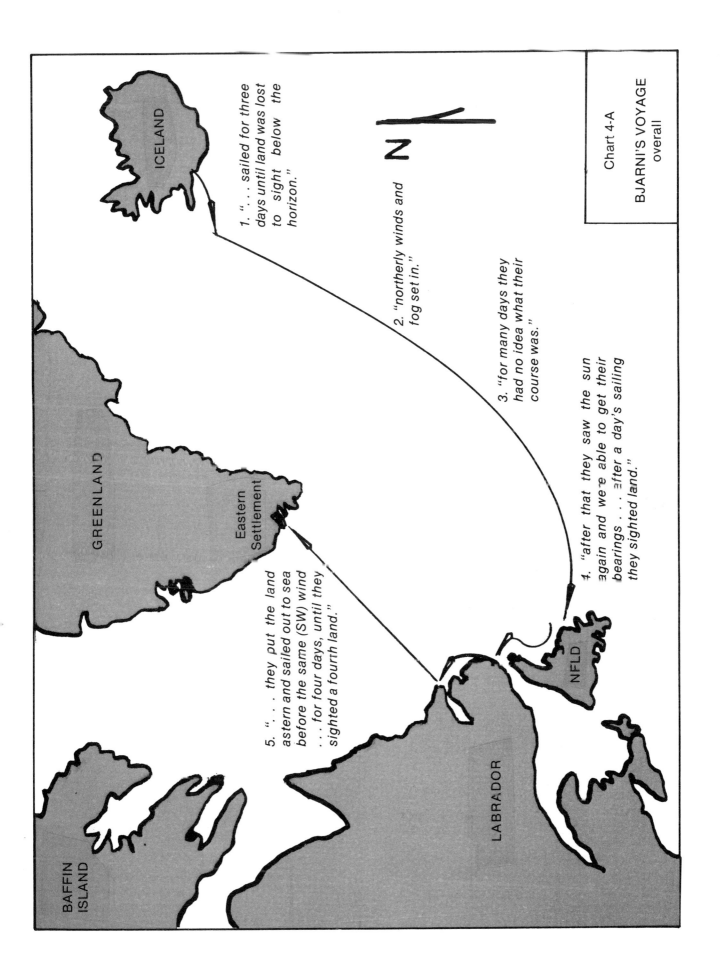

ICELAND

1. "... sailed for three days until land was lost to sight below the horizon."

N

2. "northerly winds and fog set in."

GREENLAND

Eastern Settlement

3. "for many days they had no idea what their course was."

4. "after that they saw the sun again and were able to get their bearings . . . after a day's sailing they sighted land."

5. ". . . they put the land astern and sailed out to sea before the same (SW) wind . . . for four days, until they sighted a fourth land."

BAFFIN ISLAND

LABRADOR

NFLD

Chart 4-A

BJARNI'S VOYAGE
overall

and deep with the inland end being far beyond their line of vision because of the curvature of the earth.

(D) *They closed the land quickly and saw that it was flat and wooded.*

Having followed the coast line would have meant this leg commenced in the southern part of Labrador, (below Groswater Bay) where much of it is indeed "flat and wooded."

(E) *So they put to sea again, leaving the land on the port quarter; and after sailing for two days they sighted land once more.*

The average side wind speed of 100 miles per day for two days totals 200 miles, reduced by a third for coasting; this is the distance between Southern Labrador and Newfoundland in the area of Notre Dame Bay. "Leaving land on the port quarter" refers to the left hand side of the ship and thereby indicates a northern heading against this terrain, as well as coastal voyaging. Crossing the Strait of Belle Isle accounts for sighting "land once more."

(F) *They could see that the country was not mountainous, but was well wooded and with low hills.*

An apt description of the topography of Newfoundland. Throughout known history this large island has been admired by sailors because of its timbers growing tall enough to be suitable for ships masts.

One may wonder, looking at a flat map, how Bjarni could discern the difference between the lands he had found in Newfoundland and Labrador and the coastal lands of Greenland, especially those of northern Labrador which are in the same vicinity of southernmost Greenland. Greenland is the world's largest island, and it is also quite different from any other island on earth. An ice cap covers almost all of it, with the elevation ranging up to 9,000 feet. Even in the coastal areas this ice cap is at the 5,000 foot level and above, meaning that it can been seen by a sailor at sea for 93 miles distance. The coastline is constantly indented by fjords, the side walls of which rise up vertically straight out of the sea—so straight that snow does not even cling to the sides, but instead one sees a sheer wall of grey-black-green rock whose smooth surface glistens in the sunlight. The water below is so deep that it is a dark blue even at the edge of the rock. It is one of the world's most awesomely beautiful sights. Bjarni would have had no trouble identifying it by description.

The areas which are inhabitable in Greenland are indentions into this mass of rock and ice which are quite small as indicated by the total number of farms the ancient Norse were able to establish there: 190 in two different settlements and these had to be some 300 miles apart. Within each settlement the farms were scattered along various fjords.

During World War II the Army Air Corps established an emergency landing field and named it Gardar, the name of the home of Freydis, Eric's daughter, and where the subseqent Bishopric of Greenland was located. The landing strip (and there was only one) was more comparable in length to that of a rural county airport for small planes, than to the metropolitan jet airports of today with concrete running for miles. From the pilot's standpoint, he could not fly over the field and come back in for a landing—the standard practice on approaching a landing place for the first time; and the reason was that the fjord closed in on both sides. Within these steep walls the planes simply did not have room to turn and climb out. Furthermore, he had to land headed inland, regardless of which way the wind was blowing. He had to take off seaward, which meant waiting for a favorable wind, just as the ancient mariners had to do.[15]

From a navigator's viewpoint, he had to make certain that the fjord they were entering was the right one, and had a runway at the upper end of it. All of these were "dead ends," and in a wrong approach, that term could be taken literally. One could not turn, come back out and try again. There were no road signs, but the Air Corps did help by providing moving pictures of the approach, shown at briefings to better familiarize the pilots and navigators with the situation in case they did have an emergency landing there.

Leif's Voyage

Some fifteen years after Bjarni arrived in Greenland with reports of well-wooded lands to the southwest, the Greenlanders decided upon an expedition there. A second generation was coming of age in the families of the original settlers; there was a need for additional housing, barns, ships, furniture—all of which required wood. Perhaps also there was a need for additional land inasmuch as the usable land on Greenland is quite scarce and had already been staked out. As with young people everywhere, the Saga reflects a spirit of adventure entering the picture.

Leif, the son of Eric the Red who was the leader of the Greenland colony, decided to lead the voyage (or was appointed to do so by his father, depending upon the interpretation.)

Chart #5 shows Leif's courses, and there follows here (in italics) the navigational information for these courses taken from the Saga, along with comments (in regular type).

There was now great talk of discovering new countries. Leif, the son of Eric the Red of Brattahlid went to see Bjarni Herjolfsson and bought a ship from him, and engaged a crew of thirty-five . . . They made their ship ready and put out to sea.

Brattahlid is in southern Greenland in what the Norse called their "Eastern Settlement." This area is now know as Kagassiarssuk.

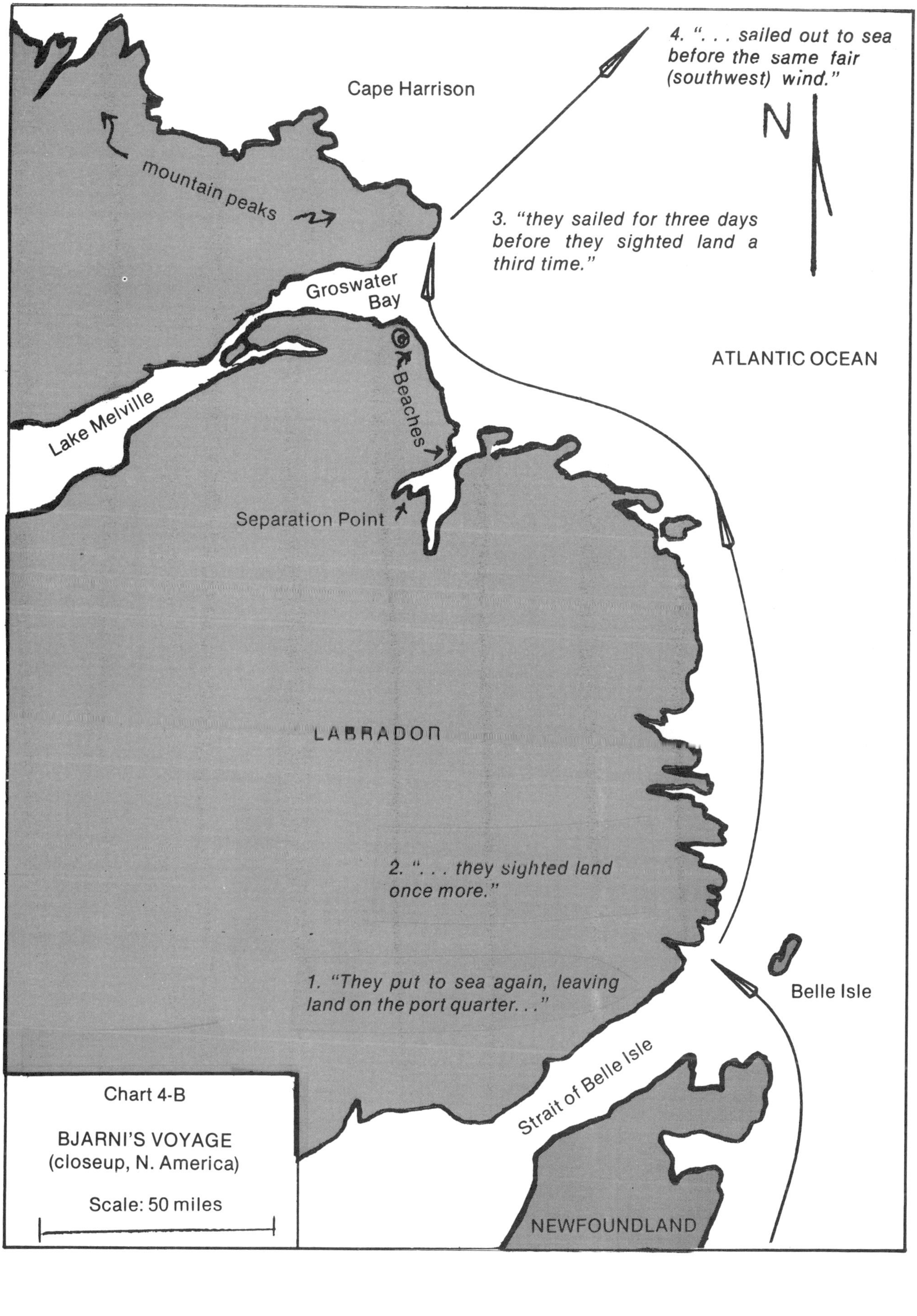

4. "... *sailed out to sea before the same fair (southwest) wind.*"

N

Cape Harrison

mountain peaks

Groswater Bay

3. "*they sailed for three days before they sighted land a third time.*"

ATLANTIC OCEAN

Lake Melville

Beaches

Separation Point

LABRADOR

2. "... *they sighted land once more.*"

1. "*They put to sea again, leaving land on the port quarter...*"

Belle Isle

Strait of Belle Isle

Chart 4-B

BJARNI'S VOYAGE
(closeup, N. America)

Scale: 50 miles

NEWFOUNDLAND

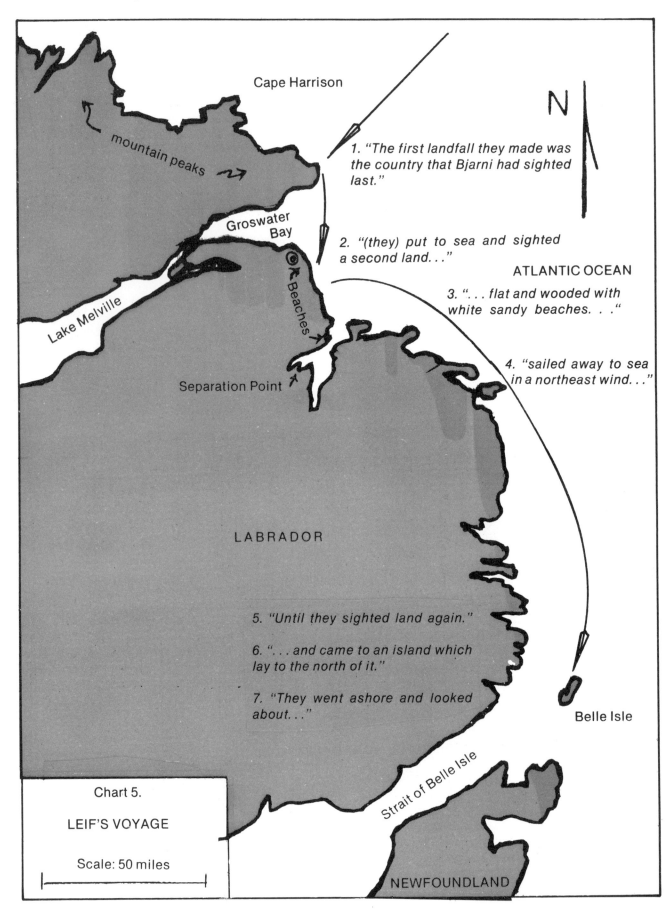

Cape Harrison

mountain peaks

Groswater Bay

1. *"The first landfall they made was the country that Bjarni had sighted last."*

N

2. *"(they) put to sea and sighted a second land..."*

ATLANTIC OCEAN

3. *"... flat and wooded with white sandy beaches..."*

Lake Melville

Beaches

4. *"sailed away to sea in a northeast wind..."*

Separation Point

LABRADOR

5. *"Until they sighted land again."*

6. *"... and came to an island which lay to the north of it."*

7. *"They went ashore and looked about..."*

Belle Isle

Strait of Belle Isle

Chart 5.

LEIF'S VOYAGE

Scale: 50 miles

NEWFOUNDLAND

The first landfall they made was the country that Bjarni had sighted last.

No sailing directions are given, except that their first landfall "was the country Bjarni sighted last," meaning they had reversed Bjarni's course.

They sailed right up to shore and cast anchor, then lowered a boat and landed. There was no grass to be seen and the hinterland was covered with great glaciers, and between the glaciers and shore the land was like one great slab of rock. It seemed to them a worthless country. Then Leif said, "Now we have done better than Bjarni where this country is concerned—we have at least set foot on it. I shall give this country a name and call it Helluland."

The description does indeed coincide with Bjarni's description of northern Labrador. The name given means "great slabs of rock." The topography of this coastline is that of a mountain range rising up "in the hinterlands," with the foothills reaching down to the sea. The elevations reach above the 2,000-foot contour, and as a consequence, are snow capped even in the summer months when Lief arrived. Technically they may not be glaciers by scientific definition, but in physical appearance with the men standing on the coastline and looking at them in the hinterland, and with their elevations being above them as well as various numbers of miles distance, it would be impossible to distinguish them from the snow-capped glaciers they had known back home in Greenland. This is an area of permafrost, in which "no grass is to be seen."

They returned to their ship and put to sea, and sighted a second land.

Again no navigational directions are given, but it is only reasonable to believe they were following Bjarni's directions and had again come to the next land enroute.

Once again they sailed right to it and cast anchor, lowered a boat and went ashore. This country was flat and wooded, with white sandy beaches wherever they went and the land sloped gently down to the sea. Leif said, "This country shall be named after its natural resources. It shall be called Markland."

The description fits southern Labrador. The word "Markland" means forest land. Here, also, there are long stretches of beach just south of Groswater Bay. This is the only place between Newfoundland and Greenland having long stretches of beaches. The bay of eighteen nautical miles width accounts for their wording "sighted a second land." By comparison, the Strait of Belle Isle is 16 nautical miles width at its mouth; and both Leif and Bjarni used the terminology of coming to another land then also (the Strait separates Newfoundland and Labrador).

They hurried back to their ship and quickly as possible sailed away to sea on a northeast wind for two days . . .

The northeast wind would have given them a side wind as they sailed southward, rounding the hump of Labrador. The two day period of sailing at 100 miles per day would carry the ship from the Groswater Bay area of Labrador down to the northern approach to Newfoundland.

. . . until they sighted land again. They sailed towards it and came to an island which lay to the north of it. They went ashore and looked about . . . then they went back to their ship and sailed into the sound that lay between the island and the headland jutting out to the north. They steered a westerly course round the headland. There were extensive shallows there and at low tide their ship was left high and dry, with the sea almost out of sight.

If our previous calculations are correct the new land they have sighted is northern Newfoundland and the "island which lay to the north of it" is the one which is now called "Belle Isle." The phrase "they went ashore and looked about" means just that: from the low sea level of the ship their visibility range is very limited. (As for example a man of average height standing on a five foot ship deck above sea level has a visibility range of only 3.8 miles.) To overcome this, sailors made it a practice to go ashore on high ground and "look about." Belle Isle is small but it rises 680 feet above sea level. This height gives it a visibility range of 30 miles, and the high ground rising up off the shores of both Newfoundland and Labrador to the 1,000-foot contour level and above adds another 36 miles, or a total visibility range of 66 miles. Now, therefore, it is possible to read a topographic map and "see" what the Norsemen saw from Belle Isle that day. To their right and the west would be the coast of Labrador extending southwestward. Along this coast is a stretch of water currently known as the "Strait of Belle Isle." The land on the other side, Newfoundland, is also rising to high ground above the 1,000-foot contour. Almost due south would be the headland they described which is now known as Cape Bauld, and in a westerly direction from this is Pistolet Bay.

As there are some smaller bays on the northern end of Newfoundland, there is a question as to which bay they entered. The Saga answers this question by telling us that "at low tide their ship was left high and dry, with the coast almost out of sight." Refer to the distance to the horizon table in Appendix B and find the same physical limitations: that is the man standing on the five foot deck would be able to see 3.8 miles. Pistolet Bay is the only one which would qualify, being some 7 miles in diameter; and therefore an observer would have the room within to see the sea disappear "almost out of sight." In each of the other cases the size of the bays is less than the visibility range of the observer.[16] Pistolet Bay also qualifies as to the other physical specification, that of having "extensive shallows."

South Labrador Coast.   The "Markland" of the Norse, which they variously described as "flat," "low," "well wooded" and "the land sloped gently down to the sea." The use of these words was by men who were accustomed to land in Greenland which rises to elevations of several thousand feet above sea level, rather sharply.

Pictured here is a section on the approach to Cartright, which is at the entrance to Sandwich Bay.

Photo by Samuel Skinner, Chief Officer, M.V. Sir Robert Bond.

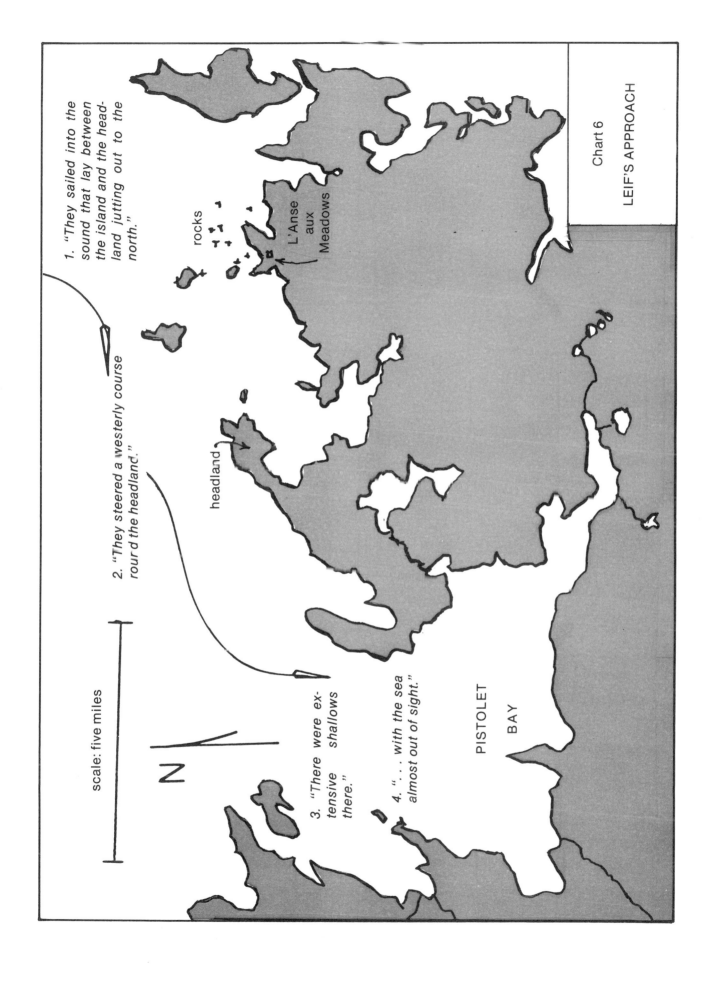

1. "They sailed into the sound that lay between the island and the headland jutting out to the north."

2. "They steered a westerly course round the headland."

3. "There were extensive shallows there."

4. "... with the sea almost out of sight."

rocks

L'Anse aux Meadows

headland

scale: five miles

N

PISTOLET BAY

Chart 6

LEIF'S APPROACH

The only other bay on the west coast of Newfoundland which fits this description is the "Bay of Islands" which is 175 miles further distance; and this simply does not fit into their description of steering "a westerly course around the headland."

They ran ashore to a place where a river flowed out of a lake.

Before proceeding to try to pinpoint locations of the Norse landing sites, the topography of the area at the time of the Norse landings needs to be understood.

Much of northwestern Newfoundland underwent land upheaval since the end of the last ice age, some eight to eleven thousand years ago. According to Mr. Norman Mercer, Mineral Exploration Consultant for the Newfoundland Department of Mines and Energy, the Northern Peninsula region of the island of Newfoundland has risen some 100 to 150 metres. It appears that the range of change for an average millennium (1000 years) is from 10 to 25 metres of uplift, but the amount of land upheaval and the range of change apparently has varied in different locations and at different time periods.

As the Norse voyages recorded in the Sagas took place nearly a thousand years ago, we need to look at a map as it would have been then.

Leif's cabins, as the Saga subsequently tells us, were located on this lake which was connected by a river to the bay. Bays are basins for the sands brought in by the sea, and therefore not subject to the same patterns of change as with the land upheavel. In this instance, the physical layout of higher ground on the Pistolet's south and east sides has not changed; and it is in a relatively protected position, not facing the ocean, but instead being behind the high ground of the promontory. So even the considerable rise in the ground itself would not likely have changed the bay. There can still be seen a wide sand bar stretching much of the way across the Pistolet at low tide.

The lake and river, however, are different matters and directly affected by the land rise inasmuch as it had to be possible for the ship to enter the lake through the river at high tide. The Norse ship was a shallow draft vessel, but even so needed some three feet of water to clear.

Now let's have a look at a map of the Pistolet Bay area. Immediately it can be seen that there is not one single possibility, but several.

As to which of the lake sites leading off of Pistolet Bay could have been the location of Leif's cabins, it becomes a question of the level of the land at the time of their landing. Not only do we have the rather wide range of uplift as stated by the geologists, but there is the further complication of the differences possible within this area. For example, at the L'Anse Aux Meadows site, those building sites are now approximately 40 feet above sea level[17] indicating a landrise of something less. But this is close to the warming waters of the ocean and is likely to have melted first with the least amount of landrise in the last millennium.

On the other hand, those sites on the southside of Pistolet Bay are located in the protective shadow of the White Hills, and some seven miles distance from the ocean, and therefore the ice cap is likely to have melted last in this area, with the bulk of its rise being most recent. The western sites appear to be the least likely inasmuch as they are located across the bay and therefore not fitting to the phrase of sailing around the headland.

The evidence, as outlined above, all points to Pistolet Bay as the bay they entered; but as to which connecting lake was the location of Leif's cabins it is impossible to say based on the information on hand. I can only point to the locale, not pinpoint the spot.

* * *

Stretching over five centuries it is possible that the L'Anse Aux Meadows site was used by more than one group of peoples during different time periods. Since five of the sixteen items tested date to the time period of Leif's voyage, could Leif have been one of those occupying the site? From the information provided by the Sagas, the answer has to be no. Here are the facts:

1. There is no river here through which the ship could have been moved. The small brook can be stepped across without getting one's feet wet.
2. There is no lake here, and instead the site is located nearby the bay. At the lower land level it would have been even closer.
3. There is a small pond up above the 50 foot contour level, but the inhabitation site is below this contour. Therefore this could not have been the tidal lake referred to in the Sagas as the house site would have been below sea level.
4. The Carbon 14 dating goes back to as early as 648 A.D. and there are ten of the instances dating at least a century prior to Leif's arrival date. The frequently published contention that this was caused by the burning of driftwood, which would account for these earlier dates, is, in my opinion, without merit. The six houses with fireplaces, the smithy and the sauna would have burned whatever driftwood there was in short order. Surely most of the wood burned would have been dated to the time of Leif's voyage, and most of the charcoals tested would have reflected this. Leif's crew was on a timbering expedition and there would have been plenty of scrap wood for the fire.

I would also object to the lumping together of the Carbon 14 dates and saying that they average around the year 1000, the time of Leif's voyage. In the first place the statement is not correct, the average is 863 A.D. Equally important is that this fails to show a period of inhabitation

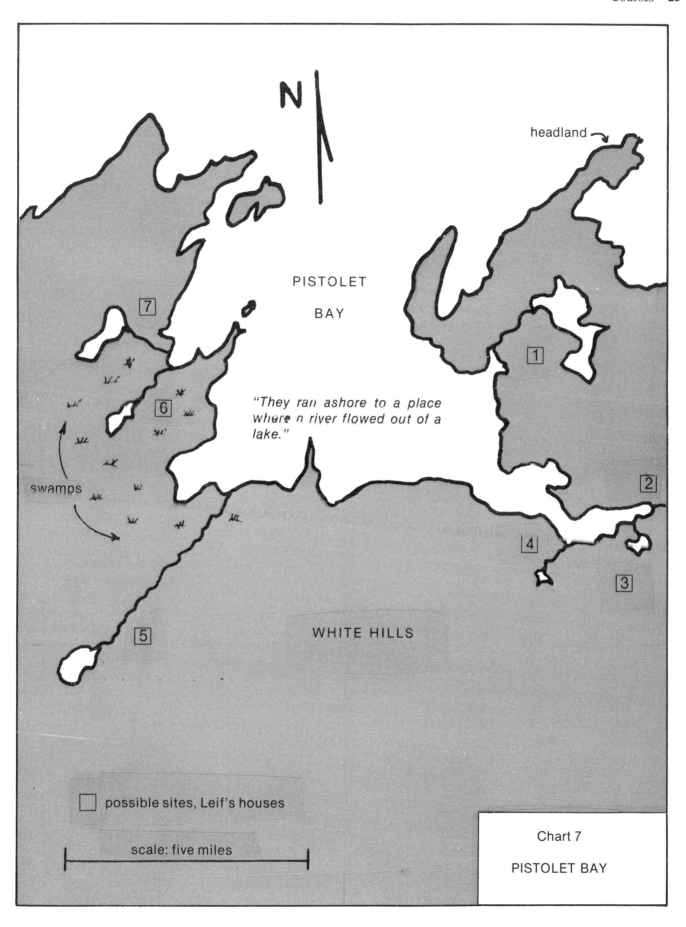

headland

PISTOLET

BAY

7

6

1

"They ran ashore to a place where a river flowed out of a lake."

swamps

2

4

3

5

WHITE HILLS

☐ possible sites, Leif's houses

scale: five miles

Chart 7

PISTOLET BAY

Tidal River, flowing from the lake (in Picture 8) into Pistolet Bay. The shallowness can be seen by the fisherman standing within it.

Photo by author.

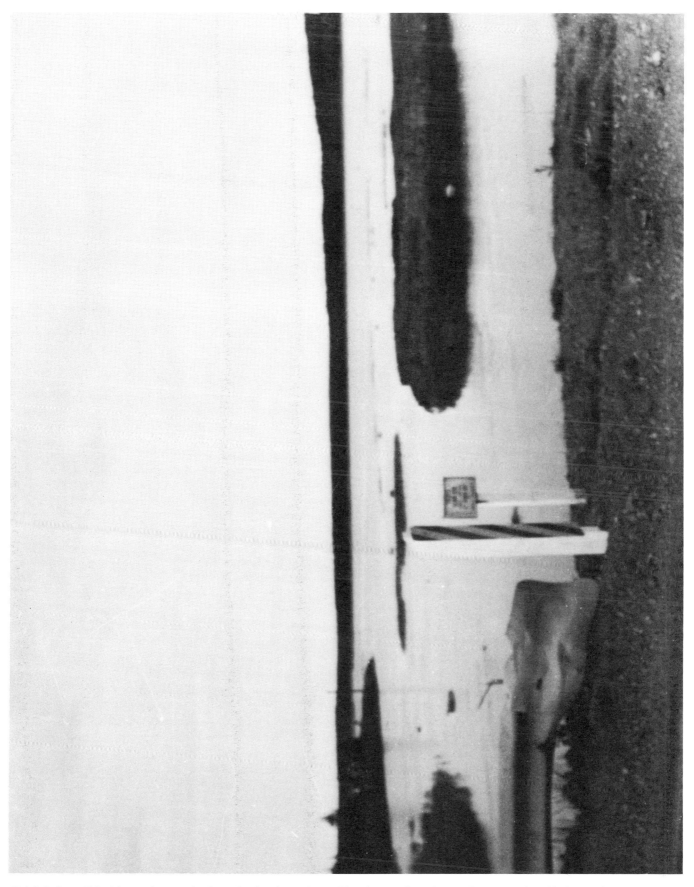

Tidal Lake. This lake outlets to the bay via the river above. The sign at the bridge rail posts notice this is a salmon river, and subject to salmon fishing regulations. The early Norse admired both the abundance and size of the salmon in Vinland.

Photo by author.

covering five centuries; Leif's visit was of one year duration, and those to whom he lent the buildings add only
five additional years.

5. The archeological site reveals a smithy with the smelting
and working of bog iron ore. Nothing is said of this in
the Sagas. Instead they spent their time cutting timber
for the ships cargo, and gathering grapes and grapevines.

*They decided to winter there and built some large houses . . .
in this country night and day were of more even length than in
either Greenland or Iceland: on the shortest day of the year, the
sun was already up by 9:00 A.M., and did not set until after 3:00
P.M. Leif named the country after its natural qualities and called
it "Vinland."*

The latitude is revealed by the time of sunrise and sunset
on December 21 which is the shortest day of the year, but
not precisely. In southern Greenland, where they had been
living, the sun rises on this date at 9:02 A.M. and sets at
2:54 P.M., local mean time; in Iceland (at 64° N.) the respective times are 9:52 and 2:04—almost an hour later in the
morning and an hour sooner in the evening. Newfoundland,
at 51° N. latitude, has a sunrise of 8:01 A.M. and sunset
of 3:55 P.M. on this date; almost an hour earlier, and later,
respectively, than at their home.

Northern Maine, Nova Scotia, and southern Newfoundland each have more than eight hours of daylight on December 21. Thus, in each of the latter cases, the sunrise statement
would be more than a full hour earlier and the sunset statement more than a full hour later. This latter fact alone
would appear to rule out speculation as to Leif Eriksson's
Vinland being located within the present United States.
Northern Newfoundland fits the phrase to within the hour.

One statement within Leif's report remains unaccounted
for: "The country seemed to them so kind that no winter
fodder would be needed for livestock; there was never any
frost all winter and the grass hardly withered at all." In
the sequence of the text this statement is made shortly after
arrival, even before finishing the houses, and they therefore
could not have known what the weather was during the
winter. The statement itself is incongruous inasmuch as it
begins talking of winter as being in the future, but ends
talking of winter being in the past. To have had "no frost
all winter" would have required a location in southernmost
Florida—even much of Florida gets occasional frost. And
nothing else in the navigation or in the content as regards
to their findings would have indicated a location so far south.

Leif himself, or the writer who eventually wrote the Saga,
may have refered to "frost" in the same manner that we
use the term "permafrost." Much of the Arctic lies in the
permafrost region. It is an area where a thin surface layer
of the earth briefly thaws each summer, but the ground
below remains frozen. Consequently, it cannot be farmed.
The northern part of Labrador is within the permafrost line,

as is Baffin Island and the other wild regions northward.
One has to come below this to find arable land, suitable
for pasturage, and where there is no *perma*-frost. This makes
the text fully in accord with the geography of the region.

Thorvald's Voyage

During the following winter, Eric the father died. In the
spring another one of his sons, Thorvald, decided to make
the trip to Vinland, having been encouraged by his brother's
success there.

*Thorvald prepared his expedition with his brother Leif's guidance
and engaged a crew of 30. When the ship was ready, they put out
to sea and there are no reports of their voyage until they reached
Leif's houses in Vinland.*

Vinland appears so easy to find that they are no longer
giving directions within the saga. The fact that they occupied
Leif's houses confirms that they did arrive there.

*There they laid up the ship and settled down for the winter, catch-
ing fish for their food. In the spring Thorvold said they should get
the ship ready and that meanwhile a small party of men should
take the ship's boat and sail west along the coast and explore that
region during the summer.*
*They found the country very attractive, with wood stretching almost
down to the shore and white sandy beaches. There were numerous
islands there, and extensive shallows. They found no traces of human
habitation or animals except on one westerly island, where they
found a wooden stack cover. That was the only man made thing
they found; and in the autumn they returned to Leif's houses.*

Earlier the Sagas had stated that Leif located his houses
along the western side of the northern headland, and it had
been found by retracing that this referred to Newfoundland.
Now, therefore, a ship "sailing west along the coast" means
sailing along the Gulf of St. Lawrence which is on the west
side of Newfoundland.

Norse ships were equipped to be rowed as well as to be
sailed and since they were using the smaller ship's boat they
could manuever in and out extensively. No waiting for the
winds to change. And it would appear that they limited
their exploration to the water routes inasmuch as they found
only one item which had been man made, a wooden stack
cover.

The World Book Encyclopedia describes the St. Lawrence
River as "This majestic stream is the largest river in Canada
and one of the largest rivers of the world. It is often called
'the Mother of Canada.' Its wide, deep waters were the first
highways of the explorers, fur traders, and colonists who
came to Canada in the early days."

Along the northern coastline there is some 700 miles distance between northern Newfoundland and present day Quebec City where the estuary narrows into a river some one

to two miles wide. It's doubtful they would have gone further because of the risk of encounter with natives in a contained area and their small crew.

The coastline itself with its indentions and jutting points may well have involved sailing in the neighborhood of 1,000 miles. Proceeding at the slowest ship's speed (see Appendix A), 75 miles per day, and sailing only every other day (with alternate days for exploring, fishing, hunting, food gathering), it would have been covered in 27 days. A direct return, at the same slow speed but without the local stops would entail one half the time.

Had they gone down the southern coast of the straits (that is the northwestern coast of Newfoundland) then they would have been involved in a journey of some 900 nautical miles which would have completely circumnavigated the island of Newfoundland. Newfoundland's coasts are far more jagged, especially in the southeastern and northeastern area and could have easily required 1,500 miles sailing to survey. Using the same minimum sailing speed of 75 miles per day, and with alternate days sailing, this could have been accomplished within 40 days.

We do know the time extent of the voyage, because they did not return until autumn. Their instructions were to explore that region during the summer.

This brings us to the third possibility: In the late spring or early summer as they began their voyage, they chose the northern coast and proceeded to the point where the river narrows; then started back along the southern coast of the Gulf. At this point they may well have believed that they were following the same shoreline as the southern shore of the Strait at Leif's village, and that this would bring them home. However, after some 300 nautical miles of sailing (or eight days' time as computed above), that shoreline began to turn south. Today this is called the Gaspé Peninsula.

Having been gone for less than half the time of their assignment, they continued southward. Thus they proceeded in a semi-circular fashion around the southwestern shores of the Gulf of St. Lawrence, which is nowadays the land of the Provinces of New Brunswick and Nova Scotia, with Prince Edward Island along the way. Some 900 miles of coast line, on an in-and-out basis, and computations on the slow sail time with alternate days of sailing would account for another 24 days en route. Then they came to the northeastern tip of Nova Scotia. The shore line turned northeastward and again the appearance was that they were headed for home. But at this point they entered a large sound with the Gulf on one side and the open ocean on the other. This is now known as "Cabot Strait."

Fourteen miles out into the Strait is the island of St. Pauls. Close enough to be seen, even at sea level from the western side, it is also high enough to see both the northern peninsula of Cape Breton Island and the southwestern peninsula of Newfoundland. Being an island there was less chance of it being occupied by any large group of unfriendly natives.

An ideal place to go and "have a look around." This approach to Newfoundland from the southwest side would thus be a repetition of Eric's (his brother's) approach to Newfoundland from the northeast side. Originally he had stopped over at Belle Isle to reconnoiter.

Here on St. Pauls, Thorvald's crew could look back and see the other side of Cape Breton tapering in the same southwesterly direction as the northern side had done along which they had just sailed. Obviously, this was the protruding peninsula of a land mass, the mountains of which could be seen inland. In the opposite direction Newfoundland could be seen. Although it is 42 miles away, the island has a height of 483 feet and the land mass on Newfoundland quickly rises above the 1,000 foot contour level, giving it a combined visibility range of 71 miles. It was in the direction of the return to their base.

Proceeding across the strait would require one day's sail, and the reconnoitering involved another day's time.

On the other side, following the same procedure of climbing the mountain they would have been able to see the range of mountains (nowadays called Long Range Mountains) which runs parallel to the west coast of Vinland/Newfoundland. Peaks along this area reach above 2,600 feet altitude and the combined visibility range for the mountains would be 109 miles. When they first started westward down the Strait of Belle Isle they would have become aware of both the shoreline extending in this direction and the mountain range lying behind it. Therefore, they deduced that Vinland was an island. They had been on their mission an estimated 62 days or a little over two months.

A polar star or sun sighting would have given them the distance in terms of difference in latitude and this would not be far off of the difference in distance of the two locations, inasmuch as the coastline has a bearing of north-northeast. Each degree of latitude represents 60 nautical miles. The latitude difference is four degrees or 240 miles; the distance "as the crow flies" between the mountain and Pistolet Bay is 270 miles.

It is also possible that they would have computed it on a dead-reckoning basis, based on the outbound part of the voyage and their journey to date. This would put them home in another 13 days, calculated as before; or a total of 75 days. From the saga it is clear that they spent at least three months on the voyage (they did not return until autumn) so my choice is, of course, based on this circumstantial evidence, that they proceeded eastward along the south shore of Vinland/Newfoundland and continued with their assignment of exploration.

Again, calculating time en route as before, the south shoreline would have been completed in approximately 13 days and the northeastern coast an estimated 14 days. Now the time enroute totals 89 days. Summer totals 91 days.

The route of this voyage of exploration is, of necessity, not certain as the Saga simply does not give enough informa-

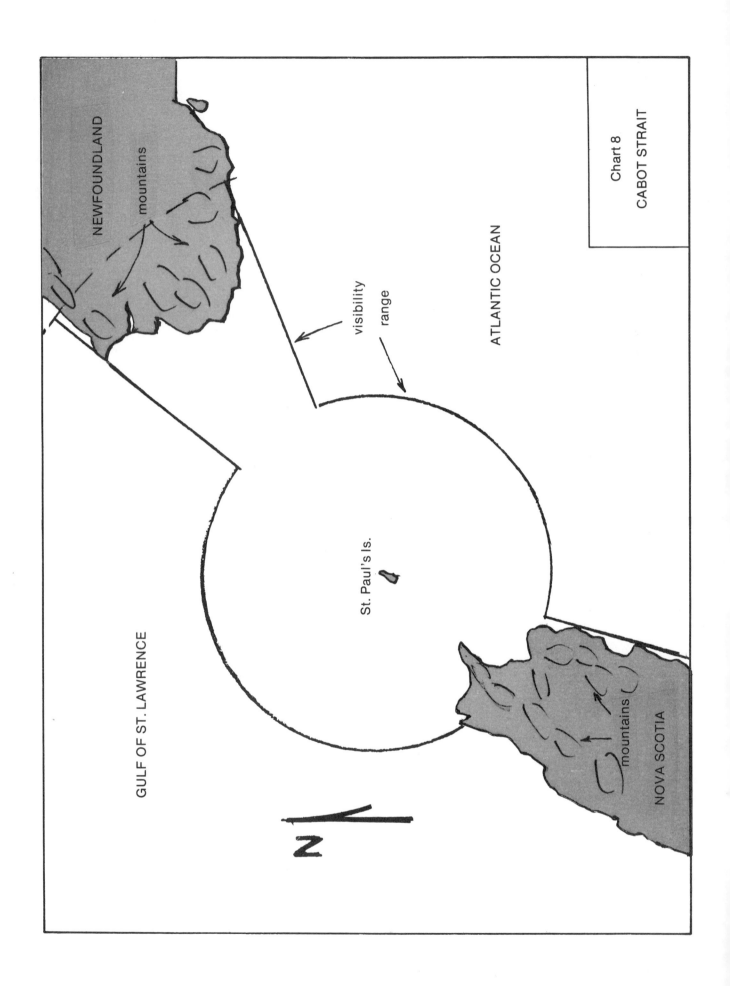

Chart 8
CABOT STRAIT

NEWFOUNDLAND

mountains

visibility range

ATLANTIC OCEAN

St. Paul's Is.

GULF OF ST. LAWRENCE

mountains

NOVA SCOTIA

N

Northern cape of Nova Scotia. Located at the tip of Cape Breton Island, this cape has a prominent land rise as can be seen in this picture, making it easily visible to St. Paul's Island in Cabot Strait.

Photo by author.

tion to make a final conclusion on it. But it is in accord with all of the information given in the Saga: It is in the prescribed direction to the west, and the coast line has to be the coast of the Gulf of St. Lawrence; there are islands at the western end of the Gulf (nearby Quebec); and the time factor does account for the entire journey within the stated time frame.

It also accounts for Adam of Bremen having known Vinland/Newfoundland was an island when he published his geography book Circa 1075 A.D., information which by his own account, he obtained from the King of the Norse people.

* * *

After having completed the above analysis on the crew's exploratory voyage, I found a report on Jacques Cartier's exploratory voyage of this same area on behalf of the French king in the year 1534. The source of this is a manuscript in the Bibliotheque Nationale in Paris, which has been translated into English in a book titled *The Discovery of North America.*[18]

Cartier was actually a Breton; but since Brittany was under the rule and made a part of France, he is usually described as a French navigator. This voyage to America is the basis of the French claim to Canada and the present settlements of Frenchmen there, principally in the Provence of Quebec which lies along both sides of the St. Lawrence River.

Fortunately, this manuscript has more detail on that voyage than we have on the earlier one by the Norse crew: the lands are described in much more detail, how they fished and hunted and found wild foods, as well as their navigation.

Cartier's ship came into Newfoundland at Cape Bonavista, and then sailed up the eastern coast of Newfoundland to the Strait of Belle Isle, and then proceeded down the West coast in a clockwise circumnavigation of the Gulf of St.

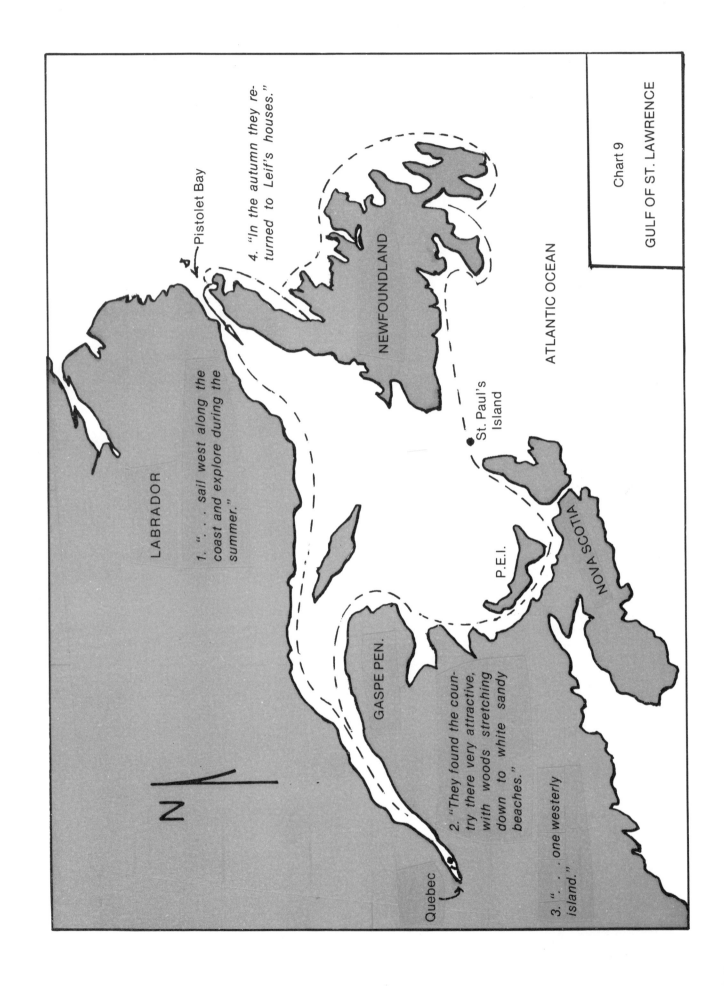

N

LABRADOR

1. "... sail west along the coast and explore during the summer."

GASPE PEN.

Quebec

2. "They found the country there very attractive, with woods stretching down to white sandy beaches."

3. "... one westerly island."

Pistolet Bay

4. "In the autumn they returned to Leif's houses."

NEWFOUNDLAND

St. Paul's Island

P.E.I.

ATLANTIC OCEAN

NOVA SCOTIA

Chart 9
GULF OF ST. LAWRENCE

Lawrence. While Thorvold's boat appears to have proceeded on its westward course in a counter-clockwise fashion, they were nonetheless involved in the same territory. The French ship would have been faster in an open sea; but Thorvald's crew had an offsetting advantage in that their boat could also be rowed, and the job of surveying the coast would dictate that they both proceed with caution at a slower speed in and out of bays and around headlands. Therefore direct comparison of the Cartier time and distance reports with that which is postulated for Thorvald is in order.

We had estimated an average of 37½ miles per day based on the slow Norse speed of 75 miles per day, and then cut this in half for the in-and-out sailings along the coastline. On the East coast Cartier covered the 203 miles distance in six days or an overall average of 34 miles per day. On the West coast of Newfoundland they proceeded from the Northern Cape down to Port au Port, a distance of 240 miles in 9 days or an average of 27 miles per day. In crossing over to Brion, Magdalen and then Prince Edward Island, they were four days en route on a course of 180 miles, or 45 miles per day average speed. No other courses lend themselves to direct measurements. The overall average for the total of 623 nautical miles in the 19 days stated for these legs gives an average of 32.8 miles per day.

But this is not the only similarity: Cartier, when reaching the Strait of Belle Isle had gone ashore and climbed the highest land in the area to reconnoiter—just as Leif had done when arriving at this same area. And just as has been postulated for Thorvald's crew in encountering an open water area at Cabot Strait. It is a common sense sailing procedure which has been practiced since time immemorial.

* * *

Continuing now with the Saga as it relates to Thorvald, nothing is said as to events later that fall or winter.

Next summer Thorvald sailed east with his ship and then north along the coast.

Coming out of Pistolet Bay they would need to sail east before turning north in order to round southern Labrador.[19] Thorvald may be giving us one more indication that his crew had already explored coastal Newfoundland around the Atlantic side, when he elected to explore northward instead of southward.

They ran into a furious gale off a headland and were driven ashore; the keel was shattered and they had to stay there for a long time while they repaired the ship.

The headland, from subsequent information, appears to have been the one on the southeast corner of Groswater Bay. Here the land quickly rises out of the sea to above the 1,000-foot contour—after having been running on a low slope down to the beach.

Thorvald said to his companions, "I want to erect the old keel here on the headland and call the place Kjalarness."

The word "ness" is a derivative of the same word as "nose" in English, and is used in the same sense that "head" is used to designate a promontory of land jutting out into the sea. "Kjal" means "keel."

They did this and then sailed away eastward along the coast. Soon they found themselves at the mouth of two fjords.

Traveling down the coast is southeastward, but the lay of the coastline in the opposite direction is westward, so that eastward distinguished their direction. One "soon" comes to what is now called Sandwich Bay. It is the mouth of two fjords with a promontory jutting out between them. This area is now called "Separation Point."

And they sailed up to the promontory that jutted out between; it was heavily wooded.

Here, within the natural basin, it is heavily wooded.

Thorvald went ashore with all his men. "It is beautiful here," he said, "here I should like to make my home."

Thorvald and his men went ashore. On their way back to their ship they encountered along the shore "three skin boats, with three men under each of them." After a violent encounter in which eight of the nine local men are killed they

returned to the headland, from which they scanned the surrounding country.

Notice how Thorvald is using the navigational technique explained earlier of going to the highland to survey the surroundings.

There next ensued an encounter with natives, in which Thorvald was fatally injured in battle.

"I advise you now to go back as soon as you can. But first I want you to take me to the headland I thought was so suitable for a home. I seem to have hit on the truth when I said that I would settle there for a while. Bury me there and put crosses at my head and feet and let the place be called Krossaness forever afterwards."

His crew followed his instructions as to his burial on the promontory which he had previously admired.

Afterwards they sailed back and joined the rest of the expedition . . . they spent the winter there and gathered grapes and vines as cargo for the ship. In the spring they set off on the voyage to Greenland; they made land at Eriksfjord and had plenty of news to tell Leif.

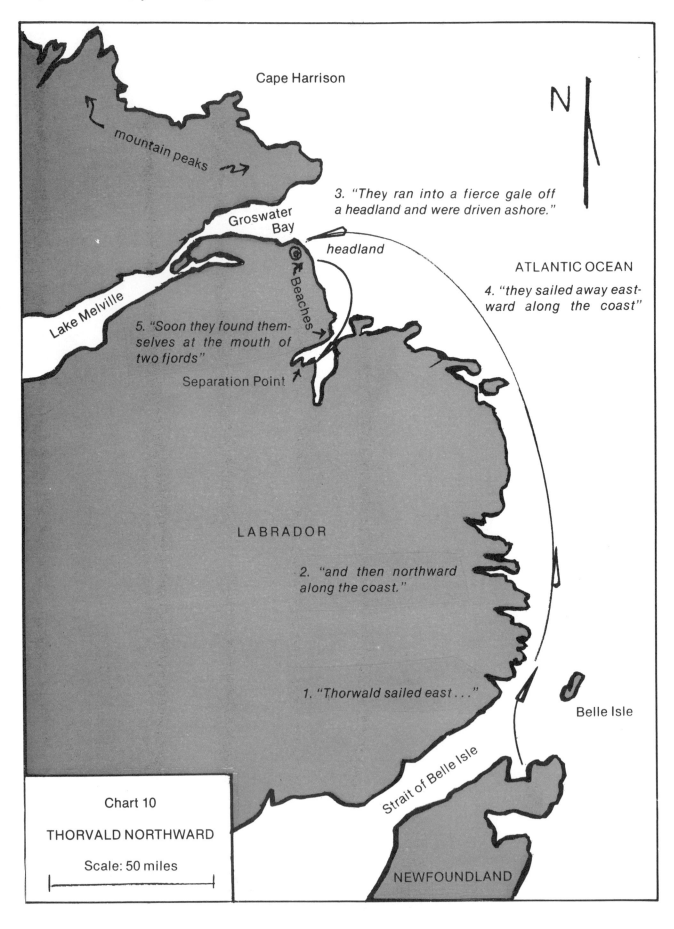

Cape Harrison

mountain peaks

Groswater Bay

3. "They ran into a fierce gale off a headland and were driven ashore."

headland

ATLANTIC OCEAN

4. "they sailed away east-ward along the coast"

Lake Melville

Beaches

5. "Soon they found them-selves at the mouth of two fjords"

Separation Point

LABRADOR

2. "and then northward along the coast."

1. "Thorwald sailed east . . ."

Belle Isle

Strait of Belle Isle

Chart 10

THORVALD NORTHWARD

Scale: 50 miles

NEWFOUNDLAND

Separation Point The "Krossaness" of the Sagas. Located off Sandwich Bay in southern Labrador, it is at the intersection of two rivers, described in the Saga as "at the mouth of two fjords . . . a promontory that jutted out between them." Thorvald said, "It is beautiful here. Here I should like to make my home."

Later, when dying, he said, "I want you to take me to the headland I thought so suitable for a home. I seemed to have hit on the truth when I said that I would settle there for a while. Bury me there and put crosses at my head and feet, and let the place be called Krossaness forever afterwards."

This picture was taken from a yacht in Sandwich Bay and gives a sea level view much as Thorvald would have had approaching the headland. The photographer was Peter Strong who wrote "We (went) there in order to fish the two great rivers that flow into Sandwich Bay on either side of the Point. It is a most interesting spot and fruitful in terms of fish: char, salmon, trout . . . The pictures do not do the place justice. An aerial photo would be much better."

I had not advised Mr. Strong the reason for requesting the photograph of this particular location but notice how his enthusiasm for it parallels that of Thorvald.

There was no problem for the crew in traveling down the coast to the Vinland colony site. It is also interesting and revealing that they later "made land at Erikstjord," meaning that they had navigated from Vinland back up to Greenland and hit their target on the button, even without their captain.

Thus, within the history of the sagas, Thorvald is the first real explorer of America. Bjarni had merely sighted the lands; Leif had landed upon them and named them, but limited his exploration to short trips which could be completed within one day.

Leif's mission was simply that of a lumberman. But Thorvald came to America for the expressed purpose of exploration and did just that. One entire season, from spring to autumn, was devoted to it; and the following spring he was back at it again.

Thorstein's Voyage

Thorstein was the third son of Eric and therefore the brother of both Leif and Thorvald. After the return of Thorvald's crew, without him, the Saga tells us:

Thorstein Ericksson was now eager to go to Vinland to fetch back the body of his brother Thorvald. He made the same ship ready and selected the biggest and strongest men available.

By going back to the area where Thorvald was killed in an encounter with the natives, and by selecting the "biggest and strongest men available," he was prepared for a fight.

When they were ready they put to sea and were soon out of sight of land. But throughout that summer they were at the mercy of the weather and never knew where they were going. Eventually, a week before winter, they made land at Lysufjord in the Western Settlement of Greenland.

Here we see the kind of problem which confronts mariners in square-rigged sailing vessels on the North Atlantic. It is a repetition of the situation which caused the turning back of eleven ships (out of 25) on Eric's voyage for the settlement of Greenland; it happened repeatedly to Brendan earlier in his efforts to achieve "the Land Promised to the Saints" over the western sea; it happened to John Cabot on his second voyage of exploration when one ship was storm tossed back to the British Isles, and the other four never heard from again; and it has happened again innumerable times both on and off the pages of history. It is simply a fact of life (or geography) that westerly winds prevail across the North Atlantic. Couple this situation with a storm and the navigator has trouble spelled with a capital "T."

The reason is not so much that the ships could not weather a storm (they did so rather admirably), but instead the navigational manuever which was necessary for them during a storm. The design of the ship itself, with a point at each end, enabled it to function much like a weather vane and thereby minimize the effects of the storms and high waves as it "ran with the sea." Its stern post spliced the thrust of waves overtaking the ship. (Unlike the later, more "modern" ships which had flat backsides and serious problems on this account.) Storms move across the Atlantic from west to east and therefore a mariner headed for the western lands is blown far off his course. Now he finds himself neither able to start a voyage with favorable winds nor able to take advantage of the prevailing westerly as a side wind (as the previous voyages from Greenland down to Newfoundland over a north-south route had been able to do). And having wound up his voyage in the Western Settlement, which is further north along the west Greenland coast, he appears to have been attempting to use the land masses which provides sailors with variable winds nearby, in order to try to achieve a crossing.

As the text states, however, this was unsuccessful. People in the Western Settlement took in the crew for the winter. Unfortunately a disease of epidemic proportions flared up in this area killing many, including Thorstein.

Thorstein's widow, Gudrid, went to stay with her brother-in-law Leif Ericksson in the Eastern Settlement. There she met a newcomer, Karlsefni, who "quickly fell in love with Gudrid and proposed to her." After receiving Leif's blessing they were betrothed.

Thorfinn Karlsefni's Voyage Begins

He spent the winter with Leif at Brattahlid . . . there was still the same talk about Vinland voyages as before, and everyone, including Gudrid, kept urging Karlsefni to make the voyage. He decided to sail and gathered a company of 60 men and 5 women . . . they took livestock of all kinds, for they intended to make a permanent settlement there if possible.

The departure point is the same as before, Brattahlid on Ericksfjord in the Eastern Settlement.

They put to sea and arrived safe and sound at Leif's houses and carried their hammocks ashore.

No sailing directions were given. This Saga briefly relates the routine work of food gathering and timber cutting. It was the following summer before they had their first encounter with the natives, and this will be discussed further in Chapter VII, Human Relations. In that same summer, Gudrid gave birth to a son and he was named Snorri. Snorri is often referred to as the "first white child born in America."

The following spring, there was a second encounter with the natives, this time ending in violence. They expected and received a third encounter in the form of a pitched battle. There are no further reports as regards the third summer.

Karlsefni spent the whole winter there, but in the spring he announced he had no reason to stay there any longer and wanted to return to Greenland . . . they put to sea and reached Ericksfjord safely.

Again these Norsemen reported no trouble in finding their way home again.

Karlsefni's Voyage According to Eric's Saga

This version is more detailed as regards the navigation of courses used and for this reason those parts are excerpted here.

There were great discussions at Brattahlid that winter about going in search of Vinland, where, it was said, there was excellent land to be had. The outcome was that Karlsefni and Snorri Thorbrandsson prepared their ship and made ready to search for Vinland that summer.

As before, this indicates a departure from Brattahlid. The statement that the search would be that summer is of significance inasmuch as the western side of Davis Strait freezes during the winter and does not thaw out until late spring or early summer. The Pilot Chart for the month of June shows the minimum ice limit as being at Resolution Island, just south of Baffin Island, and the Chart for the month of July shows both the smaller island and both major promontories of the larger Baffin Island clear of the minimum ice limit; at the same time the maximum ice limits extend as far south as northern Newfoundland.

My first experience with this phenomenon was on a ferry mission out of Goose Bay Air Base in Labrador heading for Iceland. As we went eastward I kept looking for the coastline to visually obtain a fix on the last known position before heading out to sea. The time came for the coastline to appear and it did not do so. Waiting and waiting and seeing nothing but snow underneath, things became a little hectic in the navigator's compartment as the compasses were checked and rechecked (in the far north the magnetic compass is notoriously unreliable). When the ocean appeared it finally dawned on me that I had been looking down at the ice shelf in a severe winter. The Air Corp maps did not then show this information, as the Pilot Charts now do.

They sailed first up to the Western Settlement

The western Settlement was located in the area of present day Godthaab. No reason is given for going north before turning south. It may have been simply a visit with friends or relations. Since their intention was to colonize, it seems likely that their purpose was to enlist additional colonists. In numbers there is strength and security. Karlsefni had originally started with a company of 60 men and 5 women; then in Eric's Saga it states "altogether there were 160 people taking part in this expedition."[20]

And then to Bjarn Isles.

The islands are not otherwise identified, but from subsequent information both as to distance and direction, the islands off of Baffin Island are indicated. These lie opposite the Western Settlement across the Davis Strait. It is likely that they waited for a favorable wind, a standard navigational practice in those days, and took such an easterly wind to directly cross to the lands in the west. In this manner they avoided the mistake made by Thorstein on the previous voyage. Gudrid, who had been Thorstein's wife, and was on that disastrous voyage, was now Karlsefni's wife and was also along on this voyage. She and any other member of the crew could have forwarned Karlsefni as to the problems in failing to achieve the western side of the strait before the occasional eastern winds failed.

The Hall Peninsula area of Baffin Island lies directly opposite the Western Settlement area of Greenland. A number of small islands lie off its coast, and any of these may have been named the Bear (Bjarn) Isles. This is a polar bear area.

From there they sailed before a northerly wind and after two days at sea they sighted land and rowed ashore in boats to explore it.

The northerly wind confirms the earlier hypothesis that they had waited out an easterly wind. Frontal movements moving across the Northern Hemisphere have wind patterns which shift in a counter-clockwise fashion: east, northeast, north, northwest, etc. Two days sail southward with a favorable wind at the sailing speed of 150 miles per day would bring them 300 miles from the Baffin Island area down to northern Labrador.

They found there many slabs of stone so huge that two men could stretch out on them sole to sole . . . They gave this country a name and called it "Helluland."

Since no reference is made to either a cape or a headland, it would appear that they first encountered land south of Cape Chidley, the northernmost point. Having first sailed out to sea (to avoid the dangers of the coastline area), then headed south, they would have been a bit too far east to come head on to the northern cape. The 300 miles distance covered in two days would put them in the latitude of 59° North. Here the physical description of the Saga fits the physical description of the land. While a different party is credited with naming it, the name given this country remains the same, Helluland.

From there they sailed for two days before a northerly wind and sighted land ahead.

Now begins coastwise sailing and time must be allowed for "sailing into the deep" (for safety) and return for landing.

The coastline continues in its jagged fashion, but in addition there is a continuing series of islands which are literally mountains rising out of the sea. Good sailing practice would require that they stand well off of these. Estimating a 100 mile-per-day speed because of the hazards present would bring the voyagers 200 miles further down the coast into the area of present day Hopedale. Here they have finally reached a fairly open area and one which is below the timberline.

This was a heavily wooded country . . . they named the wooded mainland itself "Markland."

Markland or "wooded land" is the same name as given in the Greenland Saga for southern Labrador. However, Karlsefni has not yet reached Groswater Bay which separates the two parts. Hopedale is on Deep Inlet, appropriately named, and inland there is a protected basin where trees

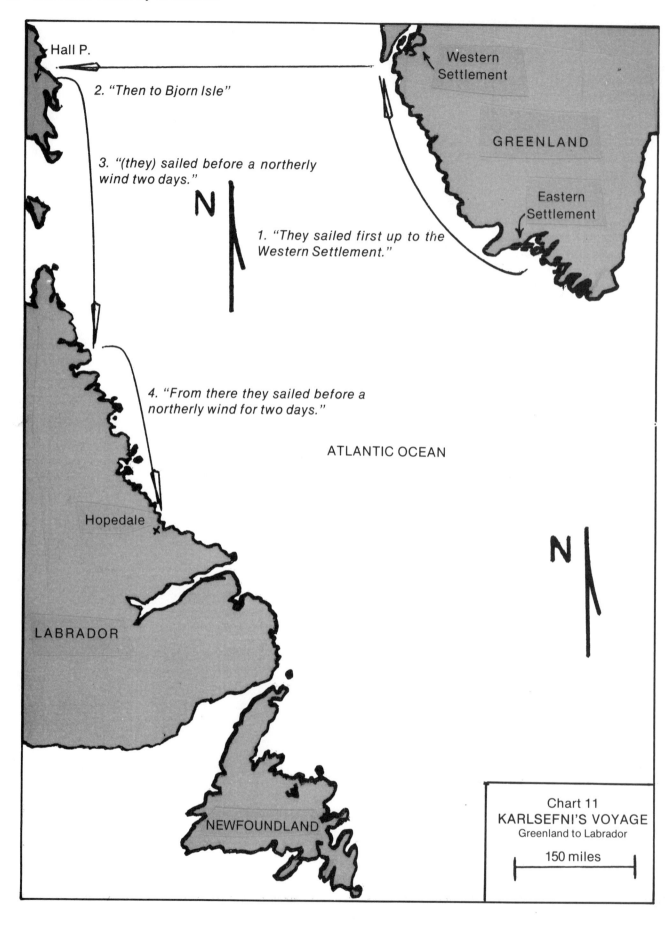

Hall P.

Western Settlement

GREENLAND

Eastern Settlement

2. "Then to Bjorn Isle"

3. "(they) sailed before a northerly wind two days."

N

1. "They sailed first up to the Western Settlement."

4. "From there they sailed before a northerly wind for two days."

ATLANTIC OCEAN

Hopedale

N

LABRADOR

NEWFOUNDLAND

Chart 11
KARLSEFNI'S VOYAGE
Greenland to Labrador

150 miles

grow to timber size. It will be noted that the Saga specifies that it is the "mainland itself" which is wooded. As he proceeds on his next leg, he'll quickly discover the coast is again barren of trees.

In the paragraph above, after the statement re the heavily wooded county, the Saga says:

There was an island to the southeast, where they found bears, and so they named it Bear Island.

Southeast of Hopedale there are many small islands which we may call "islets" and the Norse called "skerries." But there is one which is of a size to meet the description "island." This lies off Brig Harbor, above Groswater Bay, in a southeasterly direction off the land mass; and far enough off shore to make it distinctly separate—some 10 miles off the mainland. The name of it, on modern charts, is *White Bear Island.*

Of course, this may be coincidental, but there is evidence of continued contact in this area (to be discussed in Chapter VI) and, if this be the case, then a continued use of the name must be considered a possibility.

After two days they sighted land again and held in towards it; it was a promontory they were approaching. They tacked along the coast with land to the starboard.

Leaving the Hopedale area it would have been necessary to sail out and around Cape Harrison, and then the promontory below it, next they would be crossing Groswater Bay. As they do so they "sighted land again and sailed in towards it; it was a promontory they were approaching." Just such a promontory exists on the opposite shore of the bay which they were approaching. This is a little over 200 nautical miles, the distance expected in two days of coastwise sailing.

It was open and harborless, with long beaches and extensive sands. They went ashore and found a ship's keel on the headland and so they called the place "Kjalarness."

An appropriate description of the topography in the area. This is in the same area as Thorvald had identified in the Greenland Saga as "Kjalarness," and he left a keel there. It is also the same approach from the north as Leif's and their descriptions are quite similar, both as to the approach and the geography.

Then the coastline became idented with bays and they steered into one of them.

This is indeed what happens along the Atlantic coast of southern Labrador.

After three days . . . the expedition sailed on until they reached a fjord. They steered their ship into it. At its mouth lay an island

around which flowed very strong currents, and so they named it "Straum Island" . . . they steered into the fjord which they named "Straumfjord."

The strong currents are indicative of the northern branch of the St. Lawrence as it flows out to the sea through what is now called the Strait of Belle Isle. And the island at its mouth is now called Belle Isle.

They stayed there that winter, which turned out to be a very severe one; they had made no provision for it during the summer, and now they ran short of food and their hunting failed. They moved out to the island in the hope of finding game, or stranded whales, but there was little food to be found there, although their livestock throve.

Belle Isle sits out far enough to be influenced by the moderating effects of the ocean. In some winters it is encompassed by the solid ice pack and other winters it is not; and when it is not, it enjoys the warming effect of the ocean's currents which surround it.

Thorhall's Separate Voyage

They now discussed where to go . . . Thorhall the Hunter wanted to go north beyond Furdustrands (the beaches) and Kjalarness to search for Vinland there. . . .

Had they not found grapevines as yet? It must be remembered that Eric's crew had not found these originally—only when one member strayed some distance away from the others. Eric took back the vines, as well as the grapes, to make ropes. Thorvald's crew had done likewise. So it may be they cleaned out the area.

Then they put to sea and Karlsefni accompanied them as far as the island . . . with that they parted company. Thorhall and his crew sailed northward past Furdustrands and Kjalarness, and tried to beat westward from there.

Coming off Straumfjord, "the island" is again Belle Isle; turning north rounds southern Labrador; the Furdustrands, Kjalarness and Groswater Bay are in the same sequence as before; attempting to beat westward in the bay they encountered the "westerlies"—headwinds which prevail in this area. It is possible they sailed past Cape Harrison and were there trying to "beat westward." In either event, the result was the same.

But they ran into fierce headwinds and were driven right across to Ireland. There they were brutally beaten and enslaved; and there Thorhall died.

Ireland had previously been invaded by the Norsemen, who founded a number of cities there, including Dublin.

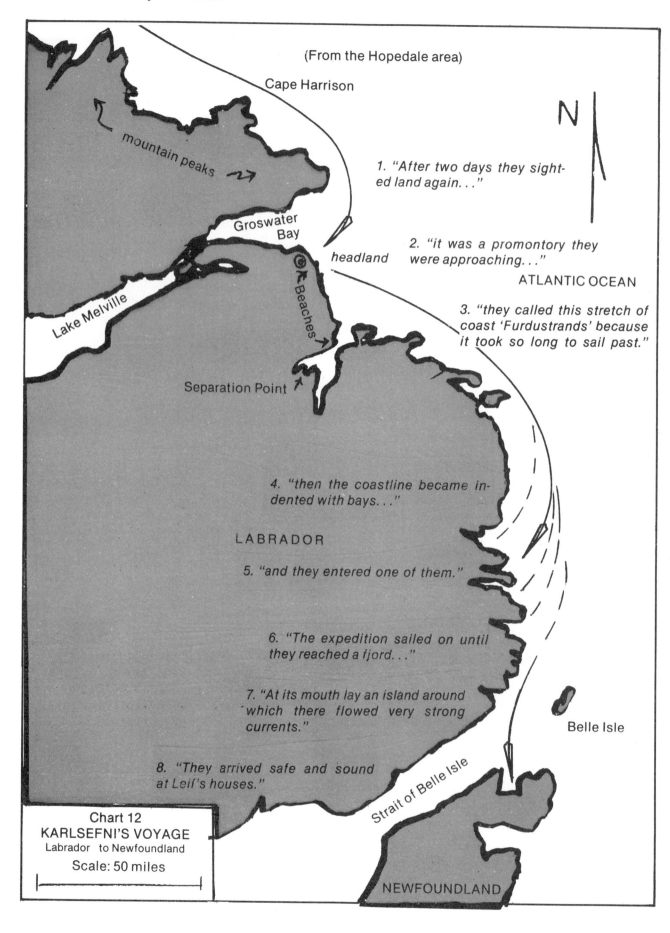

(From the Hopedale area)

Cape Harrison

mountain peaks

Groswater Bay

headland

Beaches

Lake Melville

Separation Point

1. "After two days they sighted land again..."

2. "it was a promontory they were approaching..."

ATLANTIC OCEAN

3. "they called this stretch of coast 'Furdustrands' because it took so long to sail past."

4. "then the coastline became indented with bays..."

LABRADOR

5. "and they entered one of them."

6. "The expedition sailed on until they reached a fjord..."

7. "At its mouth lay an island around which there flowed very strong currents."

8. "They arrived safe and sound at Leif's houses."

Belle Isle

Strait of Belle Isle

NEWFOUNDLAND

Chart 12
KARLSEFNI'S VOYAGE
Labrador to Newfoundland
Scale: 50 miles

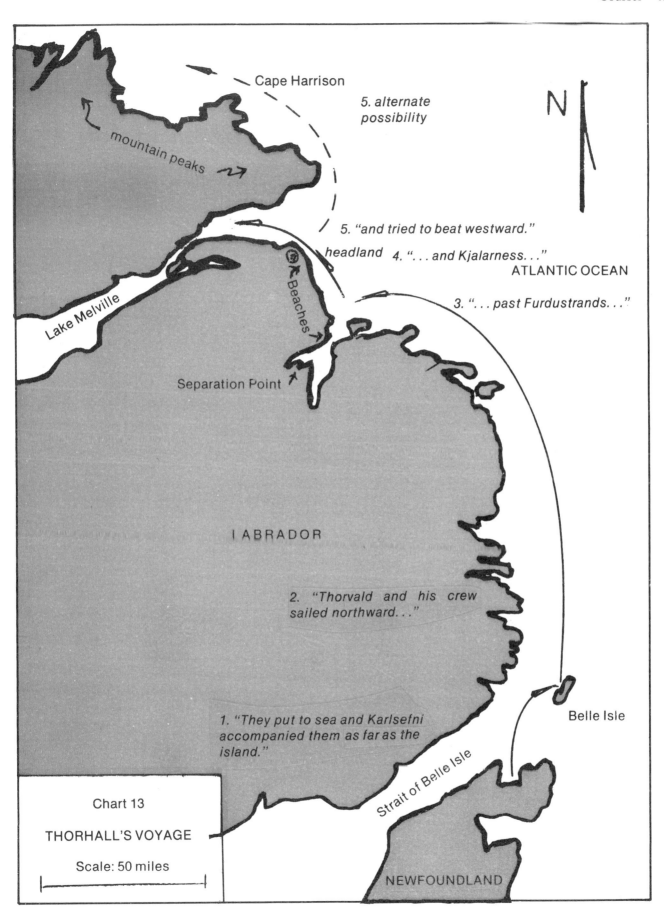

Cape Harrison

5. alternate
possibility

N

mountain peaks

5. "and tried to beat westward."

headland 4. ". . . and Kjalarness. . ."

ATLANTIC OCEAN

Beaches

3. ". . . past Furdustrands. . ."

Lake Melville

Separation Point

LABRADOR

2. "Thorvald and his crew
sailed northward. . ."

Belle Isle

1. "They put to sea and Karlsefni
accompanied them as far as the
island."

Strait of Belle Isle

Chart 13

THORHALL'S VOYAGE

Scale: 50 miles

NEWFOUNDLAND

Their first raid had occurred in the year 795, and there followed other raids, colonization and finally defeat in 1014. According to the chronology as we have reconstructed it, Thorhall would have landed in or about the year 1012. However the fighting there which led up to the final Irish victory had been going on for a number of years and the Irish were already in control of the west coast at this time. Naturally, under these circumstances, any Norseman showing up would have been poorly received.

How the information on the outcome of Thorhall's voyage reached Iceland, where the Sagas were written, is uncertain; but communications were continued through this period between Ireland and Iceland. Since Iceland was now converted to Christianity, it's possible that the report went through church sources via Rome.

Here is another example of the problem of sailing westward across the North Atlantic in the square-rigged ship. Some believe that a storm ripped off Thorhall's sail making him totally at the mercy of the currents, and these flow toward Ireland.

Karlsefni's Voyage Continuing

Karlsefni wanted to follow the coast further south, for he believed that the country would improve the further south they went . . . Karlsefni sailed south along the coast . . . they sailed for a long time and eventually came to a river that flowed down into a lake and from the lake into the sea. There were extensive sandbars outside the river mouth, and ships could only enter it at high tide.

Karlsefni, having sailed east and then south from the location on Straumfjord, has coasted down the east coast of Newfoundland. The Saga, in stating that "they sailed south along the coast" indicates that they are still on the island of Newfoundland. The land masses further south, the southern coast of Newfoundland and Nova Scotia, would require turning westward.

There are three rivers worthy of the name on the east coast of Newfoundland: the Gander, Exploits, and Terra Nova. Both the term "river estuary" and the size of Karlsefni's ship (as known from the requirements of the size of his passengar total, 65 people) require a genuine river width for passage; a stream or brook simply would not suffice.

The Terra Nova however is lacking in a wide estuary, and would require passing two headlands instead of one on return (the text only refers to one), and would require a westward heading to round the coast on return (whereas the text said they headed north).

The Exploits River's entry into the ocean is so wide that it more likely would have been called a bay, and in fact that is what it is now called on modern day charts. However, it would qualify as regards subsequent sailing directions.

The Gander River fits on all accounts: the subsequent sailing directions are properly lined up; there continue to

be extensive sandbars within the river mouth, as shown on Navigational Chart #14380; the river runs inland for some twenty miles at a width of approximately one mile which would properly be called an estuary; and there is just beyond this another sizable body of water which is today called "Gander Lake."

The text states "Karlsefni and his men had built their settlement on a slope by the lakeside" and when they had an encounter, the natives "rode away south around the headland." Assuming Karlsefni had built on the north shores facing south, as would be expected to take maximum advantage of the sun, then Gander Lake exactly fits for the natives' departure southward around the headland. The Southwest Gander River flows into Gander Lake on a northward course just to the side of the most prominent hill in the area, which immediately adjoins the lake and therefore becomes in mariner's terminology a headland.

The term "they sailed for a long time" may be accounted for by the many bays and inlets to have been explored along Newfoundland's east coast.

(they) named the place Hope . . .

Hope means a tidal lake, protected by a sand bar or other barrier. Presently Gander Lake is 82 feet above sea level, and would not qualify as a tidal lake. The tides in this area normally run only three feet with the higher tide group averaging only five feet above mean sea level. However, if the land has lifted at the higher end of the averaged scale during this last millenium in the amount of 80 feet, then Gander Lake fits precisely. Further it has a barrier at its entrance from the sea which is now in the form of low rapids. Because Gander is inland, away from the warming Atlantic currents, the ice cap here would have been later in melting, with a subsequent more rapid rise to reach its present level.

Further, Gander Lake is peculiarly well suited for a new colony. It must be remembered that commerce was by the sea and waterways in those days. So was piracy. Therefore, there was a need to be inland and not exposed to wayfarers who might sight it while sailing along the coast and be tempted to plunder. The first successful English colony in the United States, Jamestown, was located up the James River, away from the sea and even away from the beautiful harbor of Norfolk-Newport News.

The very reason we still have the remains of ancient ships in the museum at Roskilde, Demark, is that they were preserved by intentional sinking in the nearby channel; the purpose of which was to hinder and discourage a Viking raid. Thus Karlsefni and his crew found a natural barrier which would serve the same purpose. Leif had done the same thing in not locating his base on the seashore, but instead moving onto an inland lake which could be reached over a barrier at high tide. Even a Viking raider would have to think twice

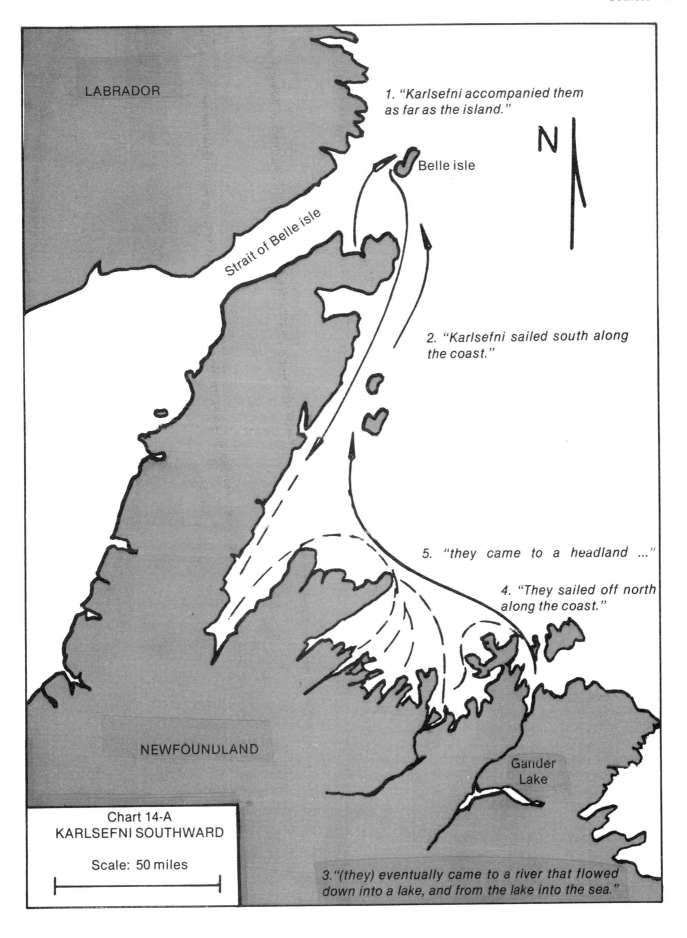

1. "Karlsefni accompanied them as far as the island."

Belle isle

2. "Karlsefni sailed south along the coast."

5. "they came to a headland ..."

4. "They sailed off north along the coast."

3."(they) eventually came to a river that flowed down into a lake, and from the lake into the sea."

LABRADOR

Strait of Belle isle

NEWFOUNDLAND

Gander Lake

Chart 14-A
KARLSEFNI SOUTHWARD

Scale: 50 miles

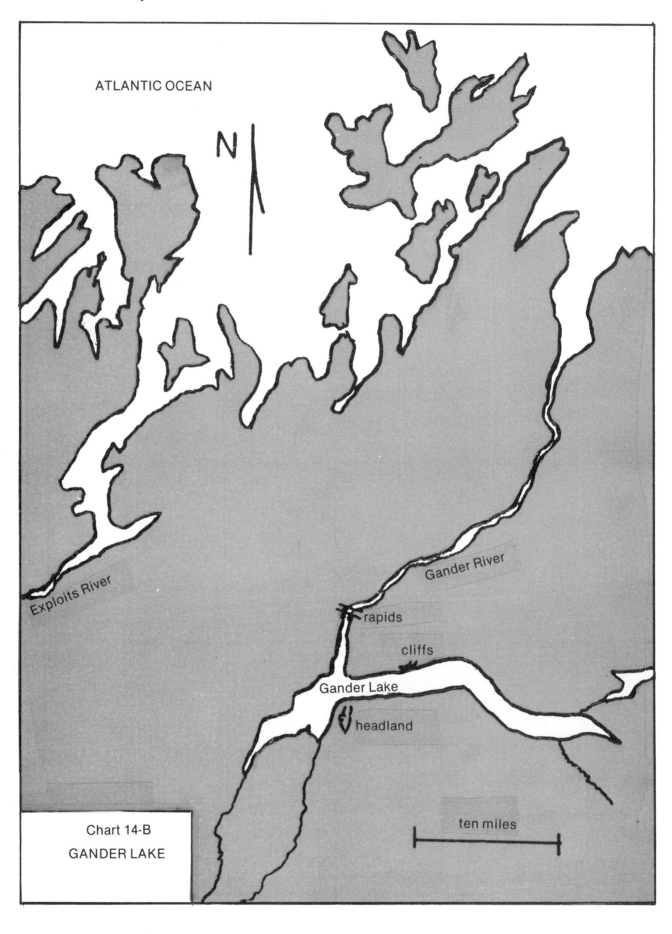

ATLANTIC OCEAN

N

Exploits River

Gander River

rapids

cliffs

Gander Lake

headland

ten miles

Chart 14-B
GANDER LAKE

before entering a tidal lake in which he may be trapped.

Gander Lake runs east and west thus providing a south facing sunny shore. No one is more aware of, or appreciative of, the sun than those who have lived in the colder climates. In Switzerland, an overall map shows that most of the villages have been built on the south slopes.

But Gander still has one more advantage: a house near the crest of the ridge on this south-facing slope could look back northward up the arm of the lake, the only entry from the sea; and thus it would function as an observation post scanning the length of the arm which runs back over four miles. Because the arm is there, a sailing ship with square rigging would be severely limited in its maneuvering ability, and may have none at all. The lookout, even if the winds favored the invader, would have plenty of time to alert the settlers.

Karlsefni could hardly have found a more secure location in terms of protection from attack from the sea, and still have access to the sea.

Here they found grapevines on all the higher ground. Every stream was teeming with fish. They dug trenches at the high tide mark and when the tide went out there were halibut trapped in the trenches. In the woods there were a great number of animals of all kinds.

But unfortunately their peace and prosperity did not last. The natives showed up—this time the ones who looked different, "evil looking." They were further described as small, with coarse hair and broad cheek bones. On the first visit they simply stared at each other; then when the natives left, "they rowed away around the south headland." On the next visit the natives "approached from the south around the headland." On this visit they proceeded to trade. But when they came back the third time, it was for a different purpose.

Karlsefni's men saw a huge number of boats coming in from the south, pouring in like a torrent . . . all the Skraelings were howling loudly . . . when they clashed there was fierce battle . . ."

Headland on Gander Lake. Each time Karlsefni commented on the arrival or departure of the natives, he referred to the headland on the south side of the lake. Here is a picture, taken from Gander Lake, of just such a headland to the south.

Photo by author.

. . . And they retreated farther up the river for they were sure that the Skraelings were attacking them from all sides. They did not halt until they reached some cliffs, where they prepared to make a resolute stand.

"Farther up the river" or moving "up stream" would mean moving along the lake in the opposite direction from the downstream route to the sea. Thus they moved toward the east, and here to the east along that south facing shore are such cliffs directly on Gander Lake.

Karlsefni and his men had realized by now that although the land was excellent they could never live there in safety or in freedom from fear, because of the native inhabitants. So they made ready to leave the place and return home. They sailed off north along the coast . . . then they came to a headland . . .

Such a headland does exist on the east coast of Newfoundland when moving up northward from the Gander Lake area toward the Strait of Belle Isle/Straumfjord. This headland is now named Cape St. Johns (not to be confused with the city of St. Johns which is in southeastern Newfoundland).

. . . soon afterward Karlsefni and his men arrived at Straumfjord.

Here is confirmation that the total distance between Hope and Straumfjord is short, as on a direct return they arrived "soon afterward."

When Leif came here, he built housing for his crew and the place was known as "Leif's houses." However, his crew had numbered only 35, whereas Karlsefni brought 160 colonists with the intention of making a permanent colony and obviously had to build additional housing. From this point on the place was given the name "Straumfjord" in the same fashion that the location of Eric's colony on Greenland is referred to as "Ericsfjord."

(Later) *Karlsefni set out with one ship in search of Thorhall. He sailed north past Kjalarness and then bore west, with the land on the port beam.*

This is confirmation of our identification of Kjalarness as being the promontory on the southeast of Groswater Bay as the coast here does bear west. There is only one other place in Labrador where the coastline bears west with land on the port beam for any appreciable distance: this is the area above Cape Harrison. The latter has to be eliminated as it does not fit the information to follow.

It was a region of wild and desolate woodland.

This is an appropriate description of middle Labrador.

When they had traveled a long way they came to a river which flowed from east to west into the sea. They steered into the river mouth and lay to by its southern bank.

There is no river along the east coast of North America which flows from east to west into the sea. However there is an unusual natural phenomenon in Labrador at Hamilton Inlet, which accounts for the appearance of a river flowing westward into a sea. Here is the Encyclopedia Britannica's description: "Lake Melville is a tidal extension of Hamilton Inlet from which it is separated by The Narrows. Averaging twelve miles in width, a depth of nearly 400 feet, it extends southwestward for 66 miles. The total length extends 150 miles." Thus one who arrives here with an incoming tide would see the water in the riverway literally runing from east to west far back into this deep and wide tidal basin, which on arrival from the east appears as a sea.

Here, within the second saga, is an account of Thorvald's death; whereas in the first saga, Thorvald was on a separate voyage but died in this area. Perhaps it is inserted at this point because they had recently been in the vicinity of Krossaness, his burial place. It had only been six years and possibly the crosses were still standing.

They reckoned that the mountains they could see roughly corresponded with those at Hope and were part of the same range, and they estimated that both regions were equidistant from Straumfjord.

Here, for the first time, we get an idea of the latitudinal location of Hope. Hamilton Inlet is located at 54° N. The parallel is 2½° above Pistolet Bay on the St. Lawrence (Straumfjord). Two and a half degrees to the south at the 49° parallel is Gander Lake, Newfoundland (Hope). See Chart 16.

Here it should also be noted that their phrase "sailed for a long time" has been used going north as well as going south. And while this does not appear to be a long distance compared to other legs of their voyages, it must be remembered that in both cases they were on search missions with the requirements of sailing in and out of the bays and coves, constantly tacking to find favorable winds to do same, and waiting out periods of both calm and unfavorable winds.

They reckoned that the mountains they could see there roughly corresponded with those at Hope.

At Gander Lake, the mountains and nearby range are at the one thousand foot elevation levels, just as they are nearby Hamilton Inlet.

They returned to Straumfjord and spent the third winter there. Quarrels broke out frequently and they decided to return to Greenland. They set sail before a southerly wind and reached Markland.

Hamilton Inlet. This is Hamilton Inlet which connects Lake Melville with Groswater Bay. To the Norse it was the "river which flowed from east to west into the sea."

The ship from which this picture was taken has just emerged from "Eskimo Passage," the narrowest section, which can be seen here off the ship's stern. The photographer was Samuel Skinner, Chief Officer aboard the M. V. Sir Robert Bond, which serves as a ferry and supply ship for Labrador.

Mr. Skinner reports the tides flow through here at three to five knots.

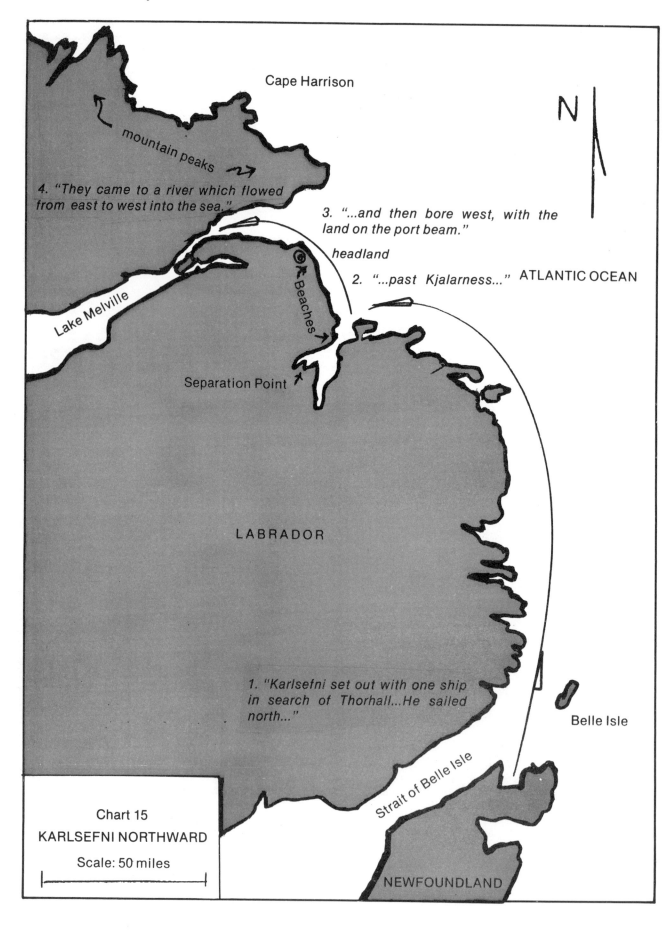

Cape Harrison

N

mountain peaks

4. *"They came to a river which flowed from east to west into the sea."*

3. *"...and then bore west, with the land on the port beam."*

headland

2. *"...past Kjalarness..."*   ATLANTIC OCEAN

Beaches

Lake Melville

Separation Point

LABRADOR

1. *"Karlsefni set out with one ship in search of Thorhall...He sailed north..."*

Belle Isle

Strait of Belle Isle

Chart 15
KARLSEFNI NORTHWARD
Scale: 50 miles

NEWFOUNDLAND

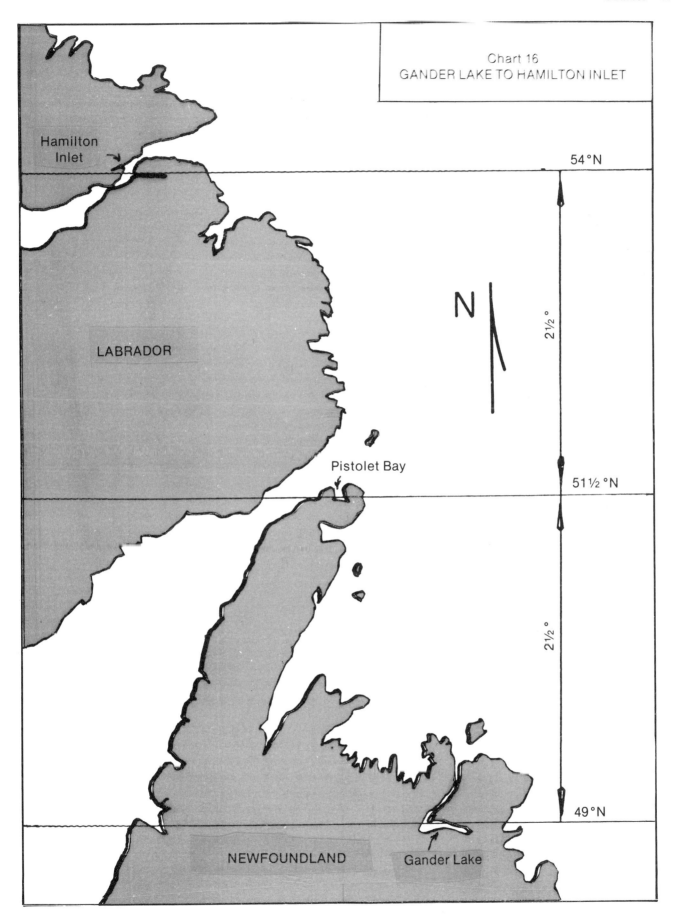

Chart 16
GANDER LAKE TO HAMILTON INLET

Hamilton
Inlet

54°N

N

2½°

LABRADOR

Pistolet Bay

51½°N

2½°

49°N

NEWFOUNDLAND   Gander Lake

Once again all accounts are in accord with Markland/Southern Labrador, lying north of Straumfjord.

Finally they reached Greenland.

Again we have no navigational information on this leg of the voyage but it is in the logical sequence and the brevity of it indicates no problem in finding their way home.

There is one piece of information remaining that does not appear to fit the solution outlined above. In describing the location of Hope, the second Saga states "they stayed there that winter. There was no snow at all, and all the livestock were able to fend for themselves." This simply would not fit the Gander Lake location as it has plenty of snow during winter.

Others have speculated that there was a warmer climate prevailing at this time period. In the prolog to the Landnamabok, which describes the settlement of Iceland during the period 870 to 930 A.D., it is stated "from Langaness to the north of Iceland it is a four-day sail to Jan Mayen Island, *at the end of the ocean.*" The U.S. Air Force navigation charts show Jan Mayen Island lying directly on the line of maximum limit of pack ice for the month of April. Thus, it is "at the end of the ocean." No substantial change in climate is indicated.

One more clue as to the general geographical location is the Norseman's identification of the fish as halibut. This is a cold water fish found in latitudes ranging from New York northward. The entire area is subject to snowfall.

The second Saga itself provides an answer:

According to some people . . . Karlsefni and Snorri had sailed south and after spending nearly two months at Hope returned that same summer.

This now makes it in accord with the first Saga with them staying at Eric's cottages all three years.

A more likely explanation of the "no snow" statement involves the rereading of the circumstances. Karlsefni had ventured forth on a colonization project, and had brought along farm animals: "They took livestock of all kinds, for they intended to make a permanent settlement there if possible."

(After landing) "They stayed there that winter, which turned out to be a very severe one; they had made no provision for it during the summer."

According to the Pilot Charts (for ship navigation) this Strait of Belle Isle is sometimes ice bound right up until June. It is on the Labrador side of the Island of Newfoundland, and therefore colder than the eastern side which faces out on the warming Atlantic. It was down the Atlantic coast that the narrative indicates Karlsefni went in turning south carrying his cattle to an area where there was now "no snow." This would have been in late spring or early summer.

This alternative reading, which is offered by the Saga itself, and is also in accord with the original Saga account, now makes the geographical location in accord with the navigational findings. However, the two Sagas themselves merit more study on this point.

First of all, the Greenland Saga does not mention any such thing happening. If this had been the case, it would have certainly been worthy of mention for its significance. Instead there is a routine statement of "the first winter passed into summer."

Now looking back to an earlier part of Eric's Saga we find the following statements: "They stayed there that winter, which turned out to be a very severe one; they had made no provision for it during the summer, and now they ran short of food and hunting failed. They moved out to the island in the hope of finding game, or stranded whales, but there was little food to be found there, although their livestock throve. Then they prayed to God to send them something to eat, but his response was not as prompt as they would have liked."

Here it relates that Thorvald the Hunter who was still a heathen believing in the god Thor, had conjured up a whale carcass with his help; that the rest of the people being Christians tried the meat, became sick, and threw the rest away. But in the Greenland Saga, which does not get into the theological argument, it simply says "soon they had plenty of good supplies, for a fine big roqual (large whale) was driven ashore; they went down and cut it up, and so there was no shortage of food."

The following spring, Karlsefni had sailed south along the east coast coming to the place called Hope which we now called Gander Lake. He did so for the stated reason "for he believed that the country would improve the further south they went."

Here they had found wild grains for the livestock, grapevines, and "every stream was teeming with fish."

As to the time element it first states "they stayed there for a fortnight, enjoying themselves, noticing nothing untoward;" then they had their encounter with the Skraelings. Here intervenes the "no snow during the winter" statement which is followed by a relation of an encounter with the Skraelings in the spring, without the use of any terminology indicating this being a return encounter or a second encounter. Instead it goes on to say that "after that there was no sign of the natives for three weeks" at which time there ensued a battle in which they were greatly outnumbered and the Norse lost two men. Karlsefni and his men had realized by now that although the land was excellent they could never live there in safety or freedom from fear, because of the native inhabitants. So they made ready to leave the place and return home." One wonders if the natives had been so profuse and the time factor had been over the period of two springs, why there had not been earlier contact?

In the very same Saga there is the additional statement,

Norse Ship From Norway. Similar to the ship in the Danish museum, pictured in Chapter II, is the Gokstad Ship, recovered from an ancient burial mound, and now located in the University Museum of National Antiquities, Oslo, Norway. Its measurements are 76½' long, 17½' abeam, the height from the bottom of the keel to the gunnel (top of side) amidship is only 6½'. Its draft (amount of water needed below to clear bottom) is only 3 feet. From the number of persons aboard Karlsefni's ship (65) it would need to have been at least this size. (Which, by the way, is by no means the largest of the Norse ships—some stretched to more than 150' in length).

We know that a Gokstad class of ship can sail the Atlantic because one has done so within modern historical times. The City of Chicago planned a Worlds Fair for the year 1892, to commemorate the fourth centennial of Columbus' discovery. Some Norwegians thought their countrymen should have been credited, so they proceeded to build a replica of the Gokstad and sailed it across the ocean.

It was Norway's exhibit at the Fair.

Photo copyright University Museum of National Antiquities, Oslo, Norway.

"according to some people Bjarni Grimolfsson . . . had stayed behind there with 100 people and gone no farther while Karlsefni and Thori had sailed south with 40 men, and after spending barely two months at Hope, had returned that same summer."

Remember that the Sagas were written down circa 1190 and 1268 A.D. the latter being 260 years after the incident had taken place and confusion about the time elements can be understandable.

If the second Saga is read as Karlsefni heading south following the severe winter, with the two encounters with the natives taking place in sequence then these combined two- and three-week periods would be in accord with the total time spent at Hope of "barely two months." Now we also see an explanation of the term "no snow" in that Karlsefni had left the place where there had been a severe winter, was looking for pastures for his livestock, and found that spring a place of "no snow."

Freydis' Voyage

Now there was new talk of voyaging to Vinland for these expeditions were considered a good source for fame and fortune . . .

One day Freydis, Eric's daughter, traveled from her home in Gardar to visit the brothers Helgi and Finnbogi. She asked them if they would join her with their ship on an expedition to Vinland, sharing equally with her all the profits that might be made from it. They agreed to this. Then she went to see her brother Leif and asked him to give her the houses he had built in Vinland; but Leif gave the same answer as before—that he was willing to lend them but not to give them away.

Gardar is nearby Brattahlid in southern Greenland and part of the Eastern Settlement.

So they put to sea, and before they left they agreed to sail in convoy if possible. There was not much distance between them, but the brothers arrived in Vinland shortly before Freydis . . .

Again the sailing from Greenland to Vinland is considered so simple, and so well understood, that no mention is made of the navigation involved.

(The brothers) had moved their cargo up to Leif's houses by the time Freydis landed. Her crew unloaded her ship and carried the cargo up to the houses. "Why have you put your stuff in here?" asked Freydis.

"Because," the brothers replied, "we had thought that the whole of our agreement would be honored."

"Leif lent these houses to me, not to you," she said.

Then Helgi said, "We brothers could never be a match for you in wickedness." They moved their possessions out and built themselves a house further inland on the bank of a lake . . .

The incident on landing was just a small preview of the troubles to follow.

Early in the spring they prepared the ship that belonged to the brothers (now dead) and loaded it with all the produce that they could get and the ship could carry. Then they put to sea. They had a good voyage and reached Ericksfjord early in the summer.

Conclusion of This Family's Voyages

This completed the fifth voyage by members of Eric's family, four of which had been successful. Every member of the family headed an expedition: the three brothers Eric, Thorvald and Thorstein, the brother-in-law Karlsefni, and even their sister Freydis. In no instance was the navigational task of finding Vinland considered too difficult for any one of them to accomplish, simply by following the instructions. In no instance did the predecessor go along with the follower, from the time of Bjarni's sighting of the land, on down through Freydis' completion of her expedition.

If one wonders why we have more information on Karlsefni's voyage than on the other four, the sagas give us an answer:

It was Karlsefni himself who told more fully than anyone else the story of all of his voyages, which has been to some extent recorded here.

If the findings presented here are correct, then these should corroborate each other. Here is a table showing locales indicated by each account within the Sagas, with the corresponding account of each other voyage whenever a physical description is given.

* * *

Karlsefni had returned to Greenland and wintered over there while Freydis was in Vinland. She returned the following summer and Karlsefni was still there when they arrived.

His ship was all ready to sail and he was only waiting for a favorable wind. It is said that no ship has ever sailed from Greenland more richly laden than the one Karlsefni commanded. He had a good voyage and reached Norway safe and sound. He spent the winter there and sold his cargo, and he and his wife were made much of by the noblest in the country.

Next spring he prepared his ship for the voyage to Iceland . . . put to sea and reached the north of Iceland, making land at Skagafjord where he laid up his ship for the winter. Next spring he bought the lands at Glaumby and made his home there; he farmed there for the rest of his life, and was considered a man of great stature.

So now we also see why the remnants of the Vinland Sagas were found in Iceland.

And so we also see how the news of the Vinland voyages was spread to Iceland and to Norway (and thence on to Denmark, we learn from the account of Adam of Bremen).

Cross Checks

	Bjarni	Leif	Thorvald	Thorhall	Karlsefni
Greenland, Description	X				
Distance to	X				
N. Labrador/Helluland Descrip.	X	X			X
Distance to	X				X
Direction to	X				X
S. Labrador/Markland Descrip.	X	X	X		X
Distance to	X	X			
Direction to	X	X	X	X	X
Vinland/Newfoundland Descrip.	X	X	X		X
Kjalarness-Furdustrands-Vinland			X	X	X

(Thorvald: Vinland/Kjalarness only)

In no instance is there a conflict.

Further breakdown on description

	Bjarni	Leif	Thorvald	Karlsefni
N. Labrador, topography	X	X		
flora		X		
S. Labrador, topography	X			
flora	X	X		
Newfoundland, topography	X	X		X
flora	X	X	X	X
fauna			X	X

All of the physical descriptions still fit these locales, with one exception: wild grapes no longer grow in northern Newfoundland.

Within the limited record of the Sagas, Bjarni Herjolfsson was the first to sight the lands to the west of Greenland;

Leif Ericksson was the first to land on them and name them;

Thorvald Ericksson was the first explorer beyond the northern cape of Newfoundland; and Thorfinn Karlsefni was the first colonist.

To the best of our knowledge no other Greenland family employed a writer to record the exploits of their forefathers. But it is not logical to believe that no one else went to Vinland. The distance was shorter, and the navigation was easier than the courses between Norway and Iceland, as well as Norway and Greenland. There was no shortage of ships among the Norse people who loved the sea and to a large extent made a living from it; witness the colonizing mission led by Eric when twenty-five vessels left Iceland. Vinland had one more thing in its favor: those who went there came back with sufficient timber, grapes and vines, and pelts to become relatively rich people in their societies. Surely something akin to "gold fever" must have stirred others in Greenland, Iceland, and back home in the Scandinavian countries.

We do have bits and pieces of information confirming that there was further voyaging and this will be discussed in chapter VII.

CHRONOLOGY OF THE COURSES

re ERIC'S FAMILY

Circa, A.D.

985	Bjarni sights western lands.
1001	Leif leaves Greenland for western lands.[21]
1003	Leif leaves Vinland, returns to Greenland.
1004	Thorvald leaves Greenland, arrives Vinland.
1005	Thorvald's crew explores Gulf of St. Lawrence.
1006	Thorvald explores Labrador/Markland, is killed.
1007	Thorvald's crew returns to Greenland.
1008	Thorstein attempts to reach Vinland, fails.
1009	Thorstein dies, Gudrid widowed.
1010	Karlsefni arrives in Greenland, marries Gudrid.
1011	Karlsefni carries colonists to Vinland.
1012	Karlsefni goes south to Hope/Gander Lake.
1013	Karlsefni spends third winter at Straumfjord.
1014	Karlsefni returns to Greenland, spends winter.
1015	Karlsefni leaves for Norway, spends winter.
1016	Karlsefni goes to Iceland, remains.
1013	Helgi and Finnbogi arrive in Greenland.
1014	Freydis and brothers go to Vinland.
1015	Freydis returns to Greenland.

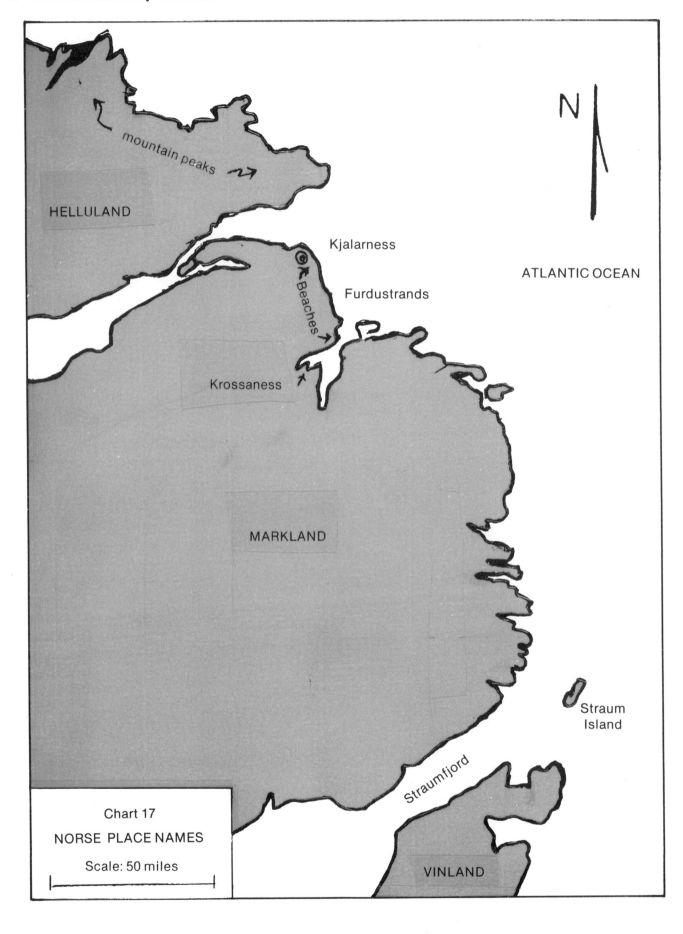

mountain peaks

HELLULAND

Kjalarness

Beaches

Furdustrands

Krossaness

ATLANTIC OCEAN

MARKLAND

Straum Island

Straumfjord

VINLAND

N

Chart 17

NORSE PLACE NAMES

Scale: 50 miles

IV

Clarifications

Grapes

One of the arguments among scholars about Vinland is the meaning of the name, and three different interpretations have been proposed: A. Grapes as we know them, B. Berries for making wine, C. A fertile land or pasture land.

As for B, berries such as the gooseberry do grow on present day Vinland/Newfoundland, and it is possible to make wine from these berries. However berries grow on bushes, and the Saga repeatedly makes clear that vines were involved. This is done at the time of the finding, "I found *vines* and grapes." "Vines" is used in relating the commodities being brought back to Greenland by Leif. And again when Karlsefni departs Vinland, they "took with them much valuable produce, *vines* and grapes and pelts."

Interpretations B and C both ignore the incident of the discovery of the grape which is told in the Saga. It relates that one of the members of the crew, Tyrkir the Southerner (Norse terminology for the Germanic peoples to the south) became separated from the others and on return he reported that he had found vines and grapes. Leif himself asked, "Is that true, foster father?"

To which the reply was, "Of course it's true. Where I was born there were plenty of vines and grapes." Germans, of course, are well acquainted with the grape, whereas the Scandinavian countries are too far north for its growth.

The Sagas go on to tell of Leif giving alternate day work assignments, between the felling of trees and the gathering of grapes and cutting of vines. It is said that the tow boat was filled with grapes. Medieval sailors carried small boats on board their ships for use as life boats, exploratory boats going into shallow waters, and sometimes as tow boats for carrying additional cargo, as in this instance.

Grapes do not grow today in Vinland/Newfoundland. But it is a matter of historical record that other explorers found them there on their arrival. Cartier, for example, on his second voyage into the Gulf of St. Lawrence, reported "also we saw many goodly vines, a thing not tofore, of us seen in those countries, and therefore we named it Bacchus Land."[22]

Grapevines, like all other vegetation, are subject to the whims of nature. It may be that a blight, such as that which wiped out the chestnut trees here in America, could have wiped out the grapevines in Newfoundland. The European grape itself was subject to just such a blight in more recent times, and the root stock there currently is the American grapevine root stock (with the European varieties grafted on). One other possible answer is that the Norse in their further explorations depleted the vines for rope making purposes. It is not necessary to move Vinland further south just to account for the grapes and the grapevines.

Skraelings

(The Norse word used for the local peoples.) There has been an ongoing argument amongst scholars as to whether this refers to Eskimos or Indians. The evidence points to most of them being neither, but instead to a third group of people—Caucasians. The evidence is both archeological-historical and physiological.

The word seems to have been applied in the Sagas to people who are outsiders in the same fashion as the Greeks referred to others as Barbarians, the Jews to others as Gentiles, and the modern American vernacular "foreigners." According to Magnusson the word "Skraeling" has an unknown derivation but is used in a contemptous sense, "something like 'wretches'."

Their first encounter with natives takes place during Thorvald's landing at Separation Point, Labrador, and the Saga makes no mention of any differences in appearance between them and the Norse. In this same area, Labrador (Markland), the subsequent expedition of Karlsefni "came upon five Skraelings—a bearded man, two women and two children." This is a significant statement because the American Indian was beardless.

The two boys were captured and carried back to Greenland. Here they described their native land as being ruled by two kings. Two "kingdoms"—or tribes—is exactly what later Europeans found in this area: The Micmacs in the south of Newfoundland and the Beothucks in the north of that island as well as further north in the Labrador area. These were two distinctly different peoples with the Micmacs being brown skinned and the Beothucks a white-skinned race.

The Sagas give more clues. Karlsefni, in returning north from Hope to Eric's cabins, both of which were on the island of Newfoundland (Vinland), came "upon five Skraelings, they reckoned that these five must be *outlaws,* and killed them." The term "outlaw" is used by the Norse in referring to their own people who had been found guilty of crimes and put outside the law—anyone could attack them and frequently did in an attitude of self protection from criminals.

Eric the Red (Leif's father) was "outlawed" out of Iceland just as his father before him had been outlawed out of Norway. The outlaw practice forced men and their families out; and as the Norse took up the land in Norway, Denmark, the Shetlands, Faeroes, and Iceland, the only open country to the west was America. The raiding by the Norse people on the outposts of Western Europe had been going on for more than two centuries by the time Karlsefni reached America. During this time men had continued to be outlawed and the only rational conclusion was that some of them reached America. The same ocean which flows between Norway and Iceland, Iceland and Greenland, also flows between Greenland and Newfoundland. The distances between each of these are approximately the same.

Karlsefni, at Hope (further south on Newfoundland), had discovered a different kind of people, and so described them: "They were small, dark colored and evil-looking and their hair was coarse and they had 'broad cheek bones'." (Doesn't every unfamiliar person appear evil looking?) Here we have a description which fits the Micmac Indians.

In contrast, back at Eric's cabins on northernmost Newfoundland, Karlsefni describes one of the Skraelings as a "tall and handsome man." In another instance, his wife Gudrid meets and talks with a native woman whose name was also Gudrid, and who was described as "pale" with "chestnut colored hair."

In an earlier encounter at this same location "the Skrael-

ings put down their packs and opened them up and offered their contents, preferably in exchange for weapons." Subsequently it is explained that these contents were furs. There would have been no reasons for Amerindians or Eskimos to trade furs—each lived in a hunting culture and furs were a by-product of their food procurement. This instance indicates foreknowledge of the practice of trading furs to people who had a need for them. On the opposite coast were the northern European peoples who valued the animal skins, were known to have traded for them, and as we have seen had the means of transport.

Karlsefni and his men had found "neither side could understand the other." The paradox may have been caused by a time factor. Today the Norwegians, the Faeroese and the Icelanders each speak a different language. Or Gudrid, the native who spoke Norse, may have been a first or second generation latecomer who still understood the mother tongue, and had intermixed with a local group.

It is also possible that these Norse People who had arrived earlier (whether or not they were outlaws) had intermixed with another group of people who were already here, the Irish/Celts, according to their own Sagas, and in turn had developed a new race, with a new language, the people who were later called Beothucks. More on this in the Ethnology section of Chapter VI.

In conclusion it would appear that the Skraelings were Micmac Indians at the southernmost location of Hope, and further north were likely to have been Beothucks.

Leif's Houses

In earlier research I came across a living example of the early Norse house still in existence at the far western end of the Island of Stromo in the Faeroes at a little village called Saxun. This building had been occupied up until ten years previously by the lady who had shown it to me. She had been born and raised there from childhood. Now it was being shown for a small fee to the occasional visitor, most of whom came there for the fishing in the bay.

The house had sides of earth built up all around it and turf was used on top, much in the same manner as pioneers in the United States had built their own turf houses. Inside at one end was the barn, separated from the people living quarters by an open slatted wall. In this fashion the heat from the animals could help warm the people inside, just as it does today in Switzerland where the farmhouse is frequently placed above the barn. At the other end of the "long house" was a stone wall serving as a combination fireplace and kitchen with all of the kitchen utensils set up there.

The floor was a surprise to me, and a pleasant one. I had always thought of dirt floors as being dirty but the Norse brought in clay for their floor which becomes hard packed and quite smooth. The surface, of this one was quite clean.

Icelandic girls' dress. Karlsefni's wife described Gudrid, the native woman, as "wearing a black, close fitting tunic." Tunics were regularly worn by Norse women as shown by this artist's batik (print on cloth) of two Icelandic girls in their native costumes.

Artist unknown.

The Norse house took advantage of nature's insulation (one which is being advocated now for the conservation of energy): six feet down into the earth the temperature is a rather constant 53°. Thus the Norse in woolen clothing with only a single fire could stay quite comfortable.

Along walls running down each side was a series of bunks "built in" in much the same fashion as a pullman train berth. Instead of curtains however they had boards which slid back and forth and the whole appearance was one of fancy cabinet work. Each sleeper thus had privacy even though they were altogether in one large room. Incidentally, it was a fight over these "bench boards" which Eric the Red had lent to another man who refused to return them which brought on his exile from Iceland, his subsequent discovery of Greenland, and from there his son's discovery of Vinland.

Now to Leif, Eric's son, and that voyage to Vinland. His crew of 35 men (on Leif's voyage no livestock is reported) could have been accommodated in two houses of 26-foot lengths based on a six-foot interval of the double bunks (bunk beds in old homes in Iceland are still smaller indicating the people were shorter at this earlier age).

My reasons for rejecting the L'Anse Aux Meadows site as the location of Leif's cabins and reasons for the selection of Pistolet Bay as the locale of Leif's cabins are stated in Chapter III. Both Thorvald's Courses and Karlsefni's Courses (all in the same Chapter) corroborate the location as regards Pistolet Bay being the area of the site.

Can Leif's houses now be found? I doubt it. These were constructed nearly a thousand years ago and by comparison we are still unable to find the first site of Jamestown, Virginia, which was settled less than 400 years ago.

A bit of L'Anse Aux Meadows remains but it was different in that it was built of sod and is in an open area. It is likely that it has been rebuilt several times as the sod wore out over its long period of occupancy. Even so, there were only ridges a few inches high visible at the time of their rediscovery. Leif's houses on the other hand were probably built of wood. They were located in a wooded area, not a grass land, and people built with the materials available to them. While the Norse wooden houses had dirt piled on the sides, they also had ditches around them for drainage, from which the dirt had been removed and piled against the house. The forces of nature would wash much of it back down into the ditches. Being in a wooded area, the site would subsequently be subjected to tree growth with roots and stumps constantly changing the surface lines over a period of ten centuries. Add to this the problem of trying to find such lines in the foliage and mulch of the scrubby woodlands which are there today. One possible hope is that Leif built in the more substantial fashion of using a wall of rocks inside the mounds of earth, thereby providing an air insulation and vapor barrier to the inner wood walls.

The Saga says they first put up booths, "then they decided to winter there and built larger houses." If so, there should be rubble piles of stone in the wall layout pattern of the houses. Provided, of course, that these have not been removed by other people for other purposes in the intervening centuries.

Vikings

The meaning of this word is "robber" and it is therefore not used to describe the people involved in these sagas. The Norse people had robbers, of course, just as other nations had and still do. But they also had farmers, fishermen, huntsmen, tradesmen, etc., and these were the people involved in these expeditions.

Vinland

The Norse people throughout their Sagas use the suffix "land" to denote a large land mass. Thus, "Iceland," "Greenland," "Helluland," "Markland," and "Vinland." Two known early geographies of the Norse and the Greenlanders use Vinland in this same context. (This is detailed later herein.)

Within the context of the Sagas, Vinland is named on Leif's voyage as a result of having found the grapes and vines while exploring inland. Note that this discovery was not made at the site of Leif's houses.

The very next voyage, that of Thorvald, Leif's brother, reiterates this same point as regards the name applying to a land mass in stating "they reached Leif's houses in Vinland." Leif's houses and Vinland were *not* one and the same.

Part of Thorvald's crew was assigned to "take the ship's boat and sail west along the coast and explore that region during the summer." They did not return until autumn to "Leif's houses." As shown in Chapter III, the summer season time span and the bits of information given indicate that their route was around the Gulf of St. Lawrence, likely returning around Newfoundland, thus identifying it as an island. Even if they had chosen the other course, westward down the shore of Newfoundland rather than Labrador-Quebec, they would still have encircled Newfoundland on a voyage of continuing exploration. The date of Thorvald's voyage is circa 1003–1004 and that voyage could account for Adam of Bremen having the knowledge that Vinland was an island when his geography was published in circa 1075.

Next we have the information contained in the voyage of Karlsefni. As he planned the trip he "asked Leif if he could have the houses in Vinland; Leif said that he was willing to lend them, but not to give them away." On arrival in Vinland they put up at Leif's houses. In the process they named this northern outlet of the St. Lawrence "Straumfjord." Fjord is the common Norse term for a waterway running to the sea from between areas of high ground.

And the Straum indicates a strong current there. Throughout Eric's Saga they refer to this as the location of Leif's houses, just as Ericksfjord in Greenland is referred to as the location of Eric's house.

When Karlsefni sailed south to a place he called Hope (identified earlier as Gander Lake), there was no indication from him that he left the same land mass. In fact to have done so would have required the crossing of a wide expanse of water, Cabot Strait off the Gulf of St. Lawrence, before reaching Nova Scotia. Even this would have to have been done in a different direction inasmuch as simply "sailing south" would have carried him far out into the Atlantic.

The finding that Hope was equidistance from Straumfjord, with Hamilton Inlet to the north confirms they were still on the same land mass.

The Greenland Saga gives a more condensed version of the Karlsefni voyage, talks in terms of their going to Vinland, and their returning from Vinland.

Vinland is the Island of Newfoundland.

V

Discovery

Discovery, like beauty, is in the eyes of the beholder.

A tourist "discovers" a new restaurant, a housewife "discovers" a new recipe, a businessman "discovers" a new source of supply.

Our history books and encyclopedias cite Eric the Red as *the* discoverer of Greenland, and Eric's son Leif as *the* discoverer of North America, usually accompanied by a statement that they were the first Europeans. But it is to the credit of the writers of the Sagas that they do not say this. Even though they are claiming discovery, they admit the prior presence of others. Eric's Saga acknowledges that Greenland had been discovered before his voyage in stating that he told his friends "he was going to search for the land that Gunnjorn had sighted when he was driven westwards off course and discovered . . ." The Landnamabok says this took place about the year 900 A.D., whereas, Eric the Red "discovered" Greenland in the year 981.

And there is still another record in the Landnamabok of an earlier colony which had been located by the Norse on the east coast of Greenland. This area has a harsher climate and the settlement there failed.

No mention is made in Eric's Saga about the previous occupation of both of the colonies he founded. These are called the Eastern and Western Settlements although both are located on the west coast of Greenland. The terms were used relative to Iceland. Another source, Ari Thorgillson's book *Icelanders,* written around 1127, states that the first Norse Settlers in Greenland had come across traces of indigenous inhabitants: "They found there human habitation, both on the eastern and western parts of the country, and fragments of skin boats and stone implements, from which it can be concluded that the people who had been there before

were of the same kind as those who inhabited Vinland and whom the Greenlanders called Skraelings."

In his book *Icelanders,* Ari tells the story of Eric's colony in Greenland through the eyes of his uncle Thorkel who had once been there and talked with original settlers. To use his exact words, "Eric the Red went there and took possession of land in the district which has since been called Ericsfjord." Eric was a man who had lived by the sword and even been driven out of Iceland because of it. The terminology of "took possession" does not jive with a peaceful finding, especially in the light of the complete omission in Eric's Saga of the presence of prior inhabitants. One wonders how much exploration work had been done by Eric in the three years spent there before bringing in the other colonists, and how much of the time was spent in "taking possession." By the evidence of the Saga, he had not spent any time on the east coast of Greenland, but on sailing there immediately turned south, then rounded the Cape and entered Ericsfjord. This was the location of Eric's first colony.

Next we come to Leif's so called "discovery" of Vinland. Again the first Saga is frank in stating that Bjarni Herjolfsson had first sighted the new lands to the west, and that Leif was going looking for them. That's the record of the Greenland Saga. But Eric's Saga, which is believed to have been written some 70 years later, amends the story to having Eric himself blown off course and first sighting the land.

Like father, like son.

The Greenland Saga relates three incidents within it, all of which indicate prior European contact with the new world. The first of these was the woman in the group of "Skraelings" who is described as "pale" (white), had "chestnut colored hair," spoke Norse, and her name was "Gudrid."

The second incident involves another person among the natives who is described as a "tall and handsome man and Karlsefni recognized that he must be their leader." The description doesn't say specifically that he looked European, but in other instances where the natives were of a different racial stock and looked different, the Saga said so.

In the third incident, on reaching Markland/Labrador, on the return, Karlsefni encountered five natives: A man, two women and two children. The man was bearded. Amerindians did not have beards as Europeans do.

The two boys were captured and brought back to Greenland. "They said that there was a country across from their own land where the people went about in white clothing and uttered loud cries and carried poles with patches of cloth attached. This is thought to have been "White Man's Land" or "Greater Ireland." The Irish had a tradition of having sailed across the sea, and of their monks going there, dating back before the time of St. Brendon in the 6th century.

On Leif's return from Vinland to Greenland he encountered another ship marooned on a reef. They rescued the crew. The leader's name was Thorir and he identified himself as a Norwegian by birth. But nothing is said about where he had been or where he came from on this trip. However, the following spring when Leif's brother planned a trip to Vinland, Thorir's cargo is revealed to be timber. This came about because Thorvald, the brother, asked for the loan of Leif's ship to which he agreed, "but first I want to send it to fetch the timber that Thorir left on the reef." Had Thorir been making the voyage from Norway, Iceland, or other parts of Europe, one would expect the cargo to have been trade goods, or if these were newcomers, household goods and supplies. Since it is raw timber, one had to suspect that his destination had been the North American mainland.

The *Geography* book of Adam of Bremen is the oldest written record of Norse voyages to Vinland, and Adam himself can be considered a neutral source—the source of his material was the King of Denmark and Norway. His statement covers two significant points.

1. That Vinland was an island, which Newfoundland is;
2. "Which had been discovered by many."

It will be noted that neither Bjarni Herjolfsson, nor Leif Ericsson, nor anyone else individually is named as the discoverer. Instead, it states plain and simply that Vinland had been discovered by many.

VI

What Ever Happened to Them?

The Norse colony in Greenland lasted more than 500 years. That's more than a century older than the oldest existing English settlement in America, and its duration more than twice that of the present United States.

Yet we have no history book relating the on-going events—only these two brief sagas which were later found as parts of other books. These deal with only two generations of a single family. The closing chapter in the Greenland Saga tells of the incentives for going to Vinland "these expeditions were considered a good source of fame and fortune." Freydis, returning from that voyage, "loaded all her companions with money." And Karlsefni, who had wintered over in Greenland before proceeding to Norway, as the Saga reports, "no ship has ever sailed from Greenland more richly laden than the one Karlsefni commanded." During the three preceding summers, Karlsefni had been in Vinland. These were ample incentives to prod men to further endeavors in America, and plenty of time in which to do it.

We have no written histories because the people taking part were not scholars. The Sagas were not written down until later. Greenland was Christianized and it would have been expected that correspondence with the Vatican would be illuminating, but unfortunately much of this was destroyed when Napoleon carried the Vatican records to France. Likewise, whatever written material which was sent back to the later capital of the Norse peoples in Copenhagen may have been destroyed by a devastating fire.

It is a situation in history akin to the Hittites, the Etruscans, and the Phoenicians wherein these people made notable achievements, and are known to us, but not through a history of their own. Almost everything we know of them comes from other sources.

The parallel to the Phoenicians is particularly striking since both they and the Norse were sea-going peoples.

The Greenland population is estimated to have reached over 3,000 based on the 280 homesteads found there.[23] In days before birth control pills, only four children surviving to maturity would mean a doubling of the numbers every generation. This population explosion had resulted earlier in the Norse movements into Britain and Ireland, taking over the Orkney, Shetland, and Faeroe Islands, then on to Iceland and Greenland. Somehow, somewhere, there had to be an outlet because Greenland's meager resources could only support so many.

The Greenland colony built an ongoing trade with Europe during these centuries for items from the North such as polar bear hides and walrus tusks. In the process its people ranged widely for hunting. But in addition to hunting for food and furs they also had to hunt for wood. Wood was used to build ships, homes, barns and furniture, as well as for fuel. Wood was necessary for their survival. Yet their home location consisted of small strips of land along narrow fjords lying at the base of glaciers; and even this land was used for pasture and farming. To the immediate west were the areas they described as the "wild lands," which were good for hunting but were above the timber line.

Where did they go to fill their ongoing needs for wood? It does not make sense that they would have sailed 1,800 miles to Norway when they knew of a source only 700 miles away. Norwegian wood would have to be purchased. Markland and Vinland trees were free for the taking.

Not only was there a difference in the distances, there was also a difference in the feasibility of the sailings. The route between Greenland and Norway has prevailing westerly winds throughout. This is great for following winds in sailing to Norway, but it makes for a long and dangerous journey on the return against headwinds. Ships outbound carrying the fur pelts would be expected to bring back the goods of the European civilization. These amounted to only two ships per year by treaty with the King of Norway when the colony came under Norwegian rule in the year 1261 A.D.

On the other hand, the north-south route between Greenland, Labrador and Newfoundland enjoyed the sailing advantage of the prevailing westerlies being side winds and therefore usable, in sailing both directions.

What evidence is there that the Norse continued their westward movement down onto the mainland of America? While there is no history book on the subject, there are fragments of history making reference to it; and in addition, four other fields of study have evidence of a Norse presence in America: geography, cartography (maps), archeology, and ethnology, the science that deals with the distinctions of mankind, their origins, speech, institutions, etc. The evidence in each of these five fields of knowledge will be here summarized.

Historical Evidence

The earliest known written reference to Vinland comes not from the Sagas but from a book written by a German Priest called Adam of Bremen around the year 1075. It states that King Svein of Denmark and Norway "recounted that there was another island in that ocean which had been discovered by many and was called Vinland, because vines grow wild there and yield excellent wine."[24] Thus we have an outsider's confirmation of the Greenlander's claim to discovery. We also have confirmation of our suspicion that Vinland was "discovered by many."

The earliest record of a Norseman in America however, antedates even Adam's account. In the year 982, Ari Marsson "one of the principal Viking Chieftains in Iceland was driven by a tempest to White Mans Land which some call Greater Ireland." It will be recalled that the Norse in the Sagas located Greater Ireland as the land beyond Vinland. Ari "could not get away . . . so was there baptised and much respected . . . was made a chief there by the inhabitants."[25]

Next comes the report of Bjorn Asbrandson who had left Iceland around the year 1000, "got a place on a ship, but of the ship nothing was heard," until another Icelander much later found him there in White Mans Land/Greater Ireland.[26]

In the year 1029 Gudlief Gudlaugson, "a great merchant" returning to Iceland from Dublin, Ireland, "met with northeast winds" and "prayed to escape from the sea." They were driven to the shores of a strange land where they found

a good harbor but were quickly surrounded by a crowd of people. The inhabitants were debating amoung themselves in the Irish language, which they understood, and the question was should the strangers be killed or kept as slaves.

While it was being discussed, "a great body of men" appeared; and with them "under a great banner" rode a tall, dignified, old man with white hair. The crowd "submitted to his decision" the fate of the strangers. The old man then "ordered Gudlief and his companions to be brought before him, and he spoke to them in the Norse language. When he found that the strangers were from Iceland, he asked many questions, especially about Kjartan, the son of Thurid of Froda.

"Then he told Gudlief it were best for him to leave at once as 'here the people are not to be trusted, and bad to deal with; and they think besides that the laws have been broken to their injury . . . there are here more powerful men than me, who little peace would give to foreigners who might come here, although they be not just here in the neighborhood where yea landed.' The old man now took a gold ring and gave it to Gudlief; then he handed him a good sword and bade Gudlief to take this sword to Kjartan of Froda, but the ring to Thurid his mother. Gudlief wanted to know who sent these valuables and the old man answered, 'if any man thinks that he knows who has owned these articles, then say these words: that I forbid anyone to come to me, for it is a most dangerous expedition . . . here is the land great . . . and in all parts may strangers expect hostility.'

"Gudlief returned to Iceland and delivered the articles and there was no doubt in anyone's mind that they had come from Bjorn Asbrandson who more than 30 years before had been a frequent visitor to the home of Thorodd and his wife Thurid of Froda. There had been much gossip and Bjorn got a place on a ship . . ."[27]

Iceland's first historian in the vernacular, Ari Thorgilsson, produced around the year 1127 a history of the Icelandic people, the *Islendingabok*. It contains a section on Greenland, but only a passing reference to Vinland: "They found there (in Greenland) human habitations, both in the eastern and western parts of the country, and fragments of skin boats and stone implements; from which it can be concluded that the people who had been there before were of the same kind as those who inhabit Vinland and whom the Greenlanders call Skraelings."[28]

The *Flatyjarbok* of Iceland was compiled in the late 1300's. In it are several fragments refering to lands in the west:[29]

1221 Eric, Bishop of Greenland went to seek Vinland.
1285 was found land west of Iceland.
1290 went Rolf about Iceland and summoned men for a new land voyage.
1347 came ship from Greenland, that had sailed to Markland, and 18 men on it.

One other source of information on the New World prior to 1492 is the Vatican in Rome. Current records there however have been substantially depleted both by paper deterioration and the scavengers who ravaged them when Napoleon carried the records to France.

We know from the Icelandic Annals that the Pope made Eric Gnupsson "Bishop of Greenland and the nearby islands" in the year 1112; and that around 1120 A.D. the Bishop set out on a visit to Vinland (this time specified by name). However the earliest Vatican records of this history is in the year 1206, and this refers to the Bishopric of Greenland.[30] Other references:[31]

1276   refers to Diocese of Garda (Greenland)

1279   refers to Garda, "as well in said island as others in same ocean." (The reference is to dispensations, and it would appear that other islands would have to include Vinland since it specifies the same ocean, and the islands back to the east were not asking for dispensation.)

1281   refers to tithes from Greenland being paid in skins of elk, musk ox, etc.—animals not to be found in Greenland, but which are native to North America.

1448   "From the natives and dwellers in Greenland a sorrowful cry has come and saddened our hearts. Barbarous people from neighboring shores sent ships to invade the island. The land was made waste with fire and sword . . ."

The Eskimo did not use swords and had no capability of manufacturing this weapon—it requires knowledge of iron smelting, which was known to the Europeans. Nor did the Eskimo travel in ships, instead they traversed these waters in small boats called kayaks (one man) and umiaks, "the woman's boat," which is family size. It would appear therefore that this was an attack by Europeans, those now living in North America (the neighboring heathen shores).

The same letter goes on to report that many of the Greenlanders were taken into slavery but later returned to their native country.

1492   Pope Alexander VI ascended to the Papacy just before Columbus sailed from Spain that year. He wrote a letter in the early years of his Pontificate as regards Greenland, but it is not clear whether this was before or after Columbus returned.[32] He states "the church of Garda is situated at the extremity of the earth in the Country of Greenland . . . on account of the rare shipping to said country due to the intense freezing of the sea no vessel is believed to have put to land there for 80 years back, or if it happened if such voyages were made, surely, it is felt that they could not have been accomplished save in the month of August, when the ice was dissolved; and since it

is likewise for 80 years, or thereabouts, absolutely no bishop or priest governed the church or personal residence, which fact, together with the absence of Catholic priests, brought it to pass that very many of the diocese unhappily repudiated their baptismal vows and since the inhabitants of that land have no relic of the Christian religion . . . the Body of Christ was consecrated by the last priest living there 100 years ago. Our predecessor wishing to provide a suitable pastor for that Church . . . appointed a bishop and pastor . . . our venerable brother Matthias. . . . at our urging (he) intending to sail personally for said Church, inspired with great fervor of devotion to lead back the souls of the strayed . . . therefore, highly commending the pious and praiseworthy undertaking of said Bishop-elect and wishing to succour him in the above circumstances, because, as we have likewise heard, he is sorely pressed by poverty . . . commit an order, in a circular letter to our esteemed sons . . . the registrars, and all the other officials . . . that under pain of excommunication, . . . all and each of the Apostolic Letters about and concerning the promotion of said Church of Garda, to be forwarded for said Bishop-elect, . . . without payment or exaction of any revenues, or even small fees . . . let it be done everywhere, because he is extremely poor."[33]

Later Norsemen would wonder how the same Pope who had divided up the New World between Spain and Portugal could have done so in the light of his prior knowledge as shown above of the Bishop of Garda, a territory which by the Vatican records included Vinland. However, the Pope was being unjustly criticed in this respect inasmuch as the Papal Bull excluded lands which had already been discovered.

Not to be overlooked are two instances in which the Sagas themselves reveal other voyaging to the western lands. The first has to do with Eric the Red wherein it states that on his exploratory mission to Greenland he spent the first summer exploring in the south, and third exploring the north and in between "he explored the wilderness to the west." West of Greenland lies Baffin Island, Labrador, and the northern part of Canada around Ungava Bay. These are all wilderness regions.

The other instance is found in Eric's Saga which was written circa 1260 A.D., with some literary embellishments. One of these has the rough character Thorhall the Hunter saying a poem as he and Karlsefni parted, the lines of which read:

"Let us head back
to our countrymen at home;
Let our ocean striding ship

explore the broad tracks of the sea
while these eager swordsmen
who laud these lands
settle in Furdustrands
and boil up whales."

The significance here is that later European peoples did do whaling in exactly this manner along the beaches of Labrador. No instance of it had previously been cited in the Sagas but this indicates that by the time of the writing, in the year 1260, it had become a practice. The open ships of that era were not equipped to handle the processing of whales as were later vessels, so the whaler needed a place on which to "beach" the animals in order to cut and "boil up" the slabs of blubber.

Previously the Greenlanders had been paying their tithes in trade goods. Listed by Bishop Eric Valdendorf these included the skins of black bear, beaver, otter, ermine, sable, wolverine and lynx, all of which are North American mainland animals and not existing in Greenland. This knowledge comes about because Valdendorf in the year 1516 planned an expedition to Greenland, and collected information on the land to the west.[34]

The western settlement of the Greenland colony was overrun in circa 1345 by Eskimos arriving from the north and west. According to their own oral history, they also conquered the eastern settlement at a later date, circa 1500.

A number of additional reasons have been put forth as to why the colony demised. These include the fact that the Norwegian King, in taking over Greenland, had originally agreed to send two ships yearly for supplies and trade, and that when the last ship was wrecked, it was not replaced—the same old problem of placing responsibility on a far away bureaucracy.

Another reason stated is that the inhabitants resented the double taxation of the church and state, and we know from the Vatican that they were having difficulty in collecting payments.

Let it be noted that the reasons for leaving Greenland are also reasons for going to the lands to the south and west, America.

In the year 1637 an Icelandic cleric-scholar Bishop Gisle Oddsson studied old documents, which were still then in existence, and concluded that the Norse in Greenland had "converted to American people."[35]

Geographical Evidence

In addition to the reference made to Vinland in the geography-history book by Adam of Bremen, circa 1075 A.D., there are two other geographies in manuscripts to be found in Iceland. One of these is a fragment believed to have been written at the end of the 14th century, which states: "South of Greenland is Helluland; next lies Markland; thence it is not far to Vinland the Good, which some think goes out from Africa; and if it be so, the sea must run in between Vinland and Markland."[36] The latter two clues are remarkable in indicating both that the land stretched far to the south, and that Vinland was an island inasmuch as "the sea must run in between."

There is further confirmation of this concept in another geography. After describing Greenland, it states that "now is to be told what lies opposite Greenland, out from the bay, which was before named Furdustrandir; there are so strong frosts that it is not habitable so far as one knows; south from thence is Helluland, which is called Skraeling Land; from thence it is not far to Vinland the Good which some think goes out from Africa; between Vinland and Greenland is Ginnungagap, which flows from the sea called Mare Oceanum, and surrounds the whole earth."[37]

As we have seen previously, the Furdustrands or Wonder Beaches are located on Markland/Labrador; the northern parts of Labrador have the permafrost and are therefore not inhabitable to farming cultures. Helluland/Northern Labrador is shown by the courses as well as by the other geography as out of sequence here which might be said to be technically correct in that the author is talking about the same land mass as Labrador; likewise the phrase "which is called Skraeling Land" is applied to a wide variety of areas as it refers to the people.

Again there is the reference to the land extending from Africa, and of course the North American coast does extend southward into the tropics. Ginnungagap is the name they gave to the present day Davis Strait, properly located; and the sea called Mare Ocean is of course the Atlantic Ocean. The final statement is one of those remarkable tidbits which indicates that the early peoples might have known a great deal more about the geography of the earth than we give them credit: it says that the ocean surrounds the whole earth, and indeed it does as we now know.

Cartographic Evidence

The earliest heretofore known map of the new world showing the lands which the Norse had discovered was drawn by Sigurdur Stefansson in the year 1570. It is shown herein. The sequence of the lands on the western side of the Atlantic is exactly the same as described in the courses: Greenland, then Helluland, Markland and Vinland.

Only the northern part of Vinland/Newfoundland is shown, but it is marked as a promontory. In addition the map has an explanatory note which says "next to them (Skraeling land) lies Vinland, which is called The Good because of the fertility of the land and its abundant produce of useful things. Our historians have wanted to make the ocean its southern boundary, but from more recent accounts I deduce that it is separated from America here by a strait or a bay."

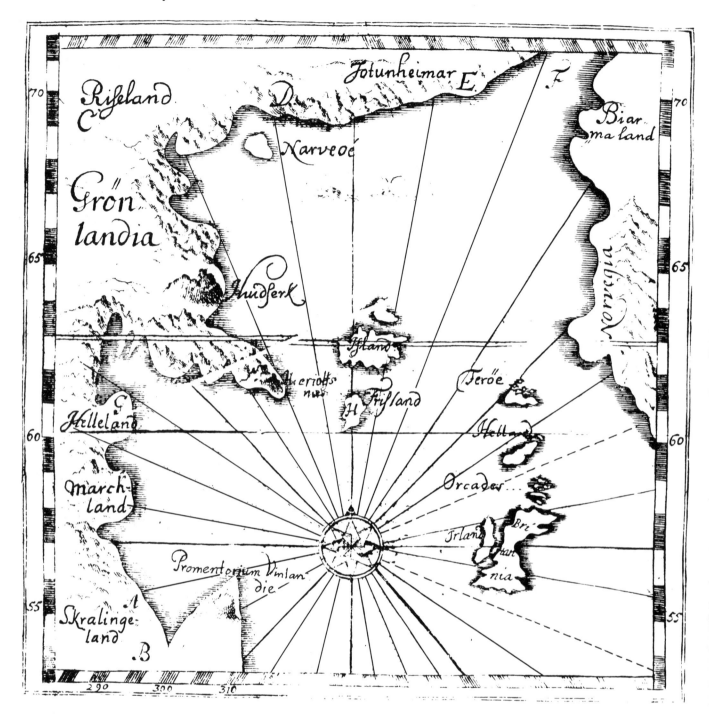

18. STEFANSSON'S MAP, 1570

Note that Helluland and Markland are separated by a bay, as at Groswater Bay; Herjolfness is at the first indention in south Greenland; and a promontory of Vinland is shown jutting out northward.

In this instance both the historians and the mapmaker are correct in that the boundary of southern Newfoundland is the ocean, and at the same time there is a separation from the mainland of America by the Gulf of St. Lawrence on the western side.

This map, like most maps, uses the terminology of the native tongue of the mapmaker. Others were calling this the Land of Corte Real, Nova Francia, New Found Land, the Estotiland (Cod Fish Land), depending upon their nationality. These were the names given by the Portuguese, French, and English, respectively; several peoples called it Cod Fish Land.

The map is drawn on a Portolan projection which has dismayed historians studying it. The latitudes, on both the European side and the American side, do not conform with the latitudes of the lands there as shown on the border scales of the map; and this is confounding because the latitudes were known to have been obtainable.

The problem may be not that the map is drawn wrong, but instead it is being read wrong.[38] Portolan means "port finding" and these were special maps drawn especially for navigators at sea. The lines radiating outward from the compass rose control it. Now look at the southern tip of Ireland, relative to the northern tip of Newfoundland and note that they are on the same relative, eastern and western radials; that is, one compass point below the median. The latitude of the southern tip of Ireland is likewise the same as the latitude of the northern tip of Newfoundland, between 51° and 52°.

This map alone is *prima facie* evidence for the Norse knowledge of the lands of northeastern America from the time of Leif Ericksson up to and through the time of the discovery by other Europeans. That knowledge is put down in black and white; and, once understood, it portrays the lands we know today as Greenland, Labrador and Northern Newfoundland.

But it is from other people that we get still earlier maps indicating the Norse presence. Giovanni da Verrazzano, an Italian, voyaged to America in 1524, exploring the eastern coast, and reporting to the King of France. (He is the man for whom the bridge in New York City is named.) On the map which was published in Rome in 1542, showing his work, there appears the designation "Norman Vilia" in the area of present day New England. This is at a coastal bay point, but the map is rather crudely drawn (which is understandable in the light of the large area covered in a short period of time) and it is not possible to say with any assurance to which bay it refers.

The same map continues on up the coast, showing Cape Breton, which is now the northeastern part of Nova Scotia. The map names it "Cavo de Brettoni," the same name which it carries even today, except we use the French spelling. Breton fisherman were living in the area. How long they had been here is unknown.

The Bretons are a Celtic people living today on the Brittany peninsula of France, which juts out to the south of England. They went there from England, where they were known as Britons. Prior to that these same Celtic peoples had first emigrated from Spain (some still remain in Galacia) sailing over the seas to Ireland; and from thence to Scotland, Wales, and England.

By both commerce and religion these people were very closely tied between Ireland-Wales-Southwest England-and Brittany. The narrow waters which lay between them were easy avenues of access, and in continuous use. Therefore one must wonder if this land called "Cape Breton" by the French and "Cavo de Brettoni" by the Italian, might not be one and the same as "Greater Ireland" to the Norse? Its geographical location is exactly the same in its relationship to Newfoundland/Vinland as both the Sagas and other Norse records stated it to be: citing first the lands to be reached from their northern positions by way of Iceland, Greenland and Labrador, then Vinland; and they say that Greater Ireland "is the land beyond Vinland." Cape Breton is directly across the strait from Newfoundland; and if one sails down the northeastern seaboard of North America, it is the land which next follows.

Verrazzano was followed 10 years later by Jacques Cartier, and the entire area was claimed for France. Since the Bretons were then subjects of the King of France in Brittany, so they were considered here. The French spelling of the name "Cape Breton" continues to this day.

But the Bretons did not originally think of themselves as French—certainly not during the period of Norse exploration into America. In fact the French government has had difficulty in getting them to speak French, a problem that has plagued them into the 20th century. They have preferred to speak in their native Celtic tongues.

The Norse, who were exploring America, were at that time also occupying Ireland and many of the Icelanders and Greenlanders had been living amoung the Irish. Therefore it would be expected that the Norse would look upon these Celts as "Irishmen."

Back to Verrazzano: In his letter report to the King of France, it becomes more apparent that the bay involved is our present Narragansett Bay in Rhode Island. Here they had received a friendly reception and enjoyed a short visit.

The natives he described as "they excel us in size; they are of bronze color, some inclining more to whiteness, and others to tawny color; the face sharply cut." He also makes reference to "we saw many breast plates wrought from copper."[39]

Another map, also Italian drawn, and published in 1556 is in a collection of travel maps by Giovanni Ramusio. It is on a smaller scale, and therefore more definitive and a bit easier to recognize. Newfoundland is shown but the Latin is used "Terra Nova"; Cape Breton is shown, and correctly as an island; the land to the north is called Terre de Labora-

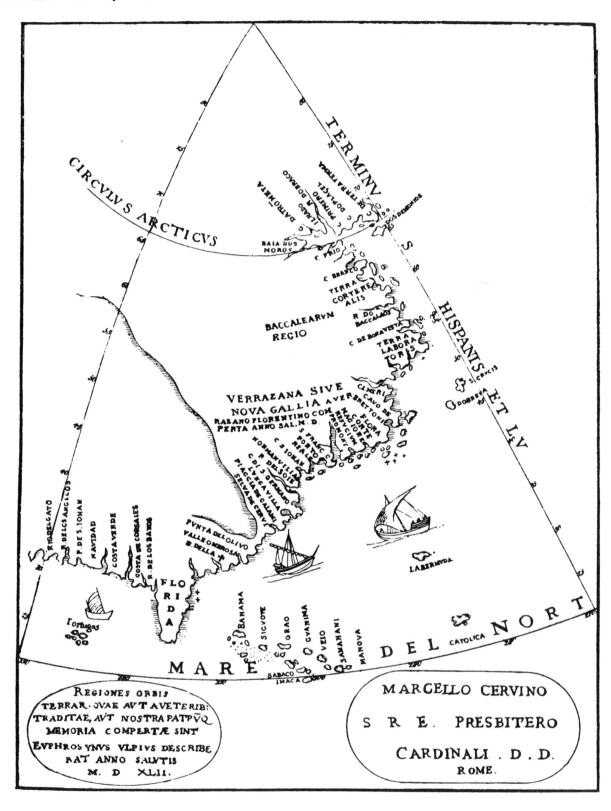

19. VERRAZANO MAP
showing "Norman vilia"

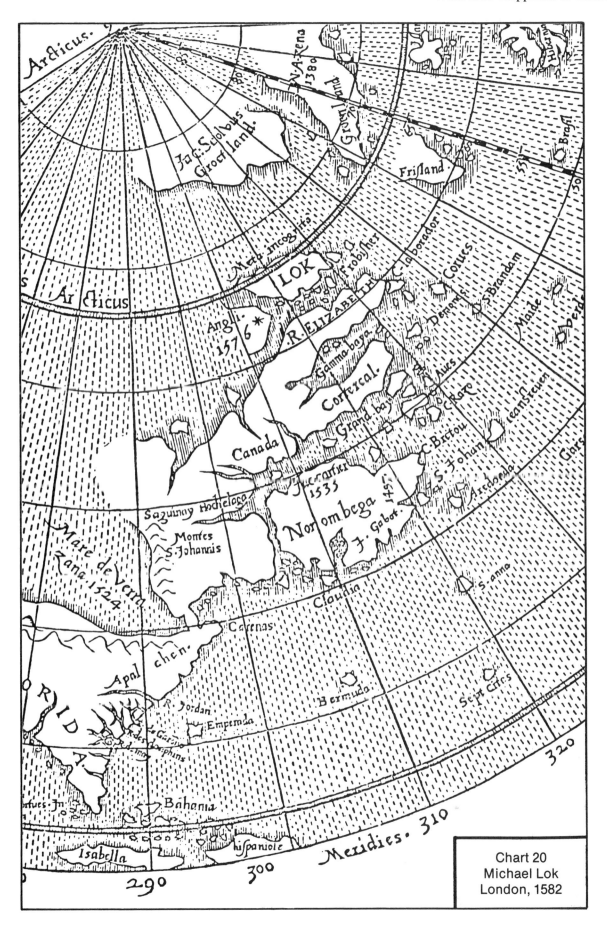

Chart 20
Michael Lok
London, 1582

dor after the Portugese explorer; the land up the St. Law-rence River is called La Nuova Francia.

Now comes the interesting part: the land between New France in the St. Lawrence Valley and the Atlantic Ocean in what we would now think of as the New England area is labeled "Terra de Nurumbega." The map uses the same terminology for the bay which Verrazzano had used, Port du Refuge (in his letter description); and the next adjoining bay uses the same title which he had used on his map "Port Real," or the King's Port.

For over a century, after the European "discoveries" in the new world and prior to the intensive settlements of these northeastern regions, the name "Norumbega" continued to be used on maps for this area. The famous mapmaker Abraham Ortelius on his map of America in 1570 so labeled it. Even after the Virginia colony was established by the English, this designation continued to be used for the New England area, and there is one map extant titled "Norumbega et Virginia."

So widespread was its usage that rare map dealer Walter Reuben refers in his catalogue to "'Norumbega,' the old name for New England."[40]

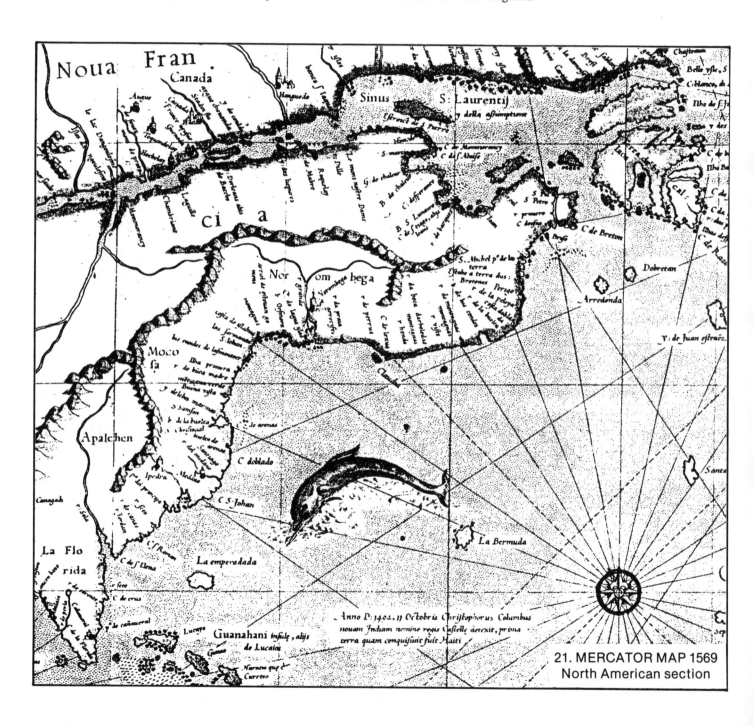

21. MERCATOR MAP 1569
North American section

Look at the Stefansson map which was not published until the year 1570. Notice how he spells Norway: "Norvegia."

But the most interesting one of all from the standpoint of a Norse study is the Mercator World Map of 1569. This is credited as being the first map to show the Appalachians as a continuous mountain range stretching parallel to the east coast. And it shows "Norombega" as the territory within that range along that part of the northeastern coast which faces to the south (as does lower New England). Naragansett Bay is more easily recognized than ever. And the name "Norombega" appears again in smaller letters adjoining the bay.

The real shock for me came when I found that the map pictures a European type medieval tower at this location.

That tower still stands in Newport, Rhode Island and will be discussed further in the next section.

Oddly enough, this appears on a map done by one of the most famous mapmakers of all time, Gerald Mercator, but appears to have been completely overlooked until now. It is on his map of 1569, and the English Colony at Plymouth (Massachusetts) was not settled until the following century in 1620. A picture of a blown-up section of the map is shown here and the reader can judge for himself how well drawn and located was the Newport Tower. Compare this to the pictures of the tower in the section to follow, bearing in mind that the stucco is now weathered away from the stone walls, the third floor level and roof have been blown off, and there is no present adjoining structure.

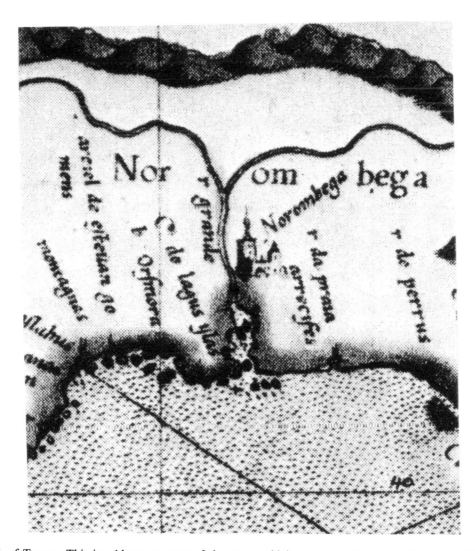

Mapmakers Sketch of Tower. This is a blown-up copy of the tower which appears at Narragansett Bay on Mercator's World Map of 1569 some 67 years before the English settled in Rhode Island in 1636.

Gerald Mercator.

Newport Tower. As it appears today, after the stucco has weathered away from its stone walls, the roof and part of the third floor blown off.

Photo by author.

Fireplace and Window.   Each is so placed that the fire casts a beam of light down the Newport ship channel.

Photo by author.

Archeological Evidence

Most widespread, and the most disputed, evidence of pre-Columbian Norse presence in America is in the field of archeology. Artifacts have literally been found all the way from Ungava Bay at the northern tip of Labrador and Quebec all the way down into the United States. The question is which, if any, of these are genuine and which are fake.

On two of these some navigational knowledge might help in resolving the impasses which exist between proponents and opponents.

Newport Tower

The first of these is the most visible of the artifacts in question. This is the stone tower in Newport, Rhode Island. There are lots of theories about its origin with many arguing that it came into existence during Colonial times. However Dr. Clyde Keeler points out that a letter petition requesting a land grant refers to the territory already containing the stone tower.[41] It was written before the English Colonial period began in that location.

Two researchers, working independently, came up with the same findings as regards the construction of the tower.[42] It had been built on the Rhineland foot as the unit of measure (12.35 modern inches). This unit was in use in the low countries and Scandinavia during the period of time involved in the Norse exploration of America. Both the diameters of the columns and the diameters of the structure itself measured from the column centers are divisible into whole numbers of feet by this measurement.

From a navigator's standpoint the most interesting study is one done by a civil engineer, Edward A. Richardson, and recorded in a scientific journal.[43] He uses schematic drawings to show that the place for the fireplace on the second floor, along with a window placed opposite it, carried the beam of light from the fireplace directly down the channel entrance of the harbor.

The fireplace which uses one of the columns as a flue had to have been precisely placed for this purpose. The same is true of the opposite window.

The building also has a window on the second floor which is south facing. This serves as a lookout over the Atlantic which is visible out to 11.4 nautical miles and could alert people in the tower to approaching ships who would then have to come around Newport Neck in order to enter the harbor. The design of this structure leaves little room for doubt that it was constructed for navigational purposes by maritime people using the ocean.

But it may also have been used for other purposes. It may have simultaneously served as a round tower church, as some of the edifices in Norway and elsewhere have done. There are recesses within the inside walls similar to those built in churches for statuary. Religious buildings in seaports have long had the dual function of being lighthouses and/or landmarks for the sailor.

Thirdly, the solid construction of the building makes it apparent that it was also intended as a stronghold. In the petition referred to above the references to the tower say that it could be occupied and serve the soldiers and men as a trading post while dealing with "the savages." It was so well built that the British used it during the Revolutionary War and later tried to blow it up, but could only succeed in taking off the roof and a few feet of the upper floor.[44]

Windows on higher levels were smaller and similar to those found in defensive strongholds elsewhere.

The question has been raised as to why Verrazzano, on his visit here, did not report it. That which is reported on his and his brother's maps may be a word description of the picture which is drawn on Mercator's map: Norman Vilia. Norman is the French word for Norseman and therefore would have been the language of the French king to whom he was reporting. Villa in both French and Italian means a country house or estate.

The earliest known English map of the area, drawn in 1634, designates this site as "Old Plymouth." This was to differentiate it from "New Plymouth" in Massachusetts where the Pilgrims had settled. The word "old" in this context should certainly need no further elaboration. As to their calling it "Plymouth," they were in the process of claiming it.[45]

Spirit Pond Stone

One more piece of archeological evidence to which a navigational interpretation may add some knowledge is in one of the so-called "Spirit Pond" stones, named for the location where they were found in southern Maine. Herewith is both a photographic picture of the stone and a drawing making the diagram easier to read.

The Spirit Pond stones demonstrate a problem for archeologists in the study of Pre-Columbian American history. Paper, wood, and other materials, even including iron, deteriorate into dust with time. The lower quality of the iron instruments made in earlier times left them without resistance to oxidation. Stones have the advantage of being permanent, at least within the time spans involved here. As the old Indian saying goes: "Only stones live forever."

In spite of their permanence, the carved stones have a scientific limitation: they cannot be Carbon 14 dated. Archeologists have therefore turned to linguists, to try to ascertain dating time periods, as well as the language being used by the inscribers. But this is not an exact science as we will soon see.

Factors which are usually taken into consideration are: the script, the words themselves and the question of when they came into use in the language, the spelling of the words, and the grammar.

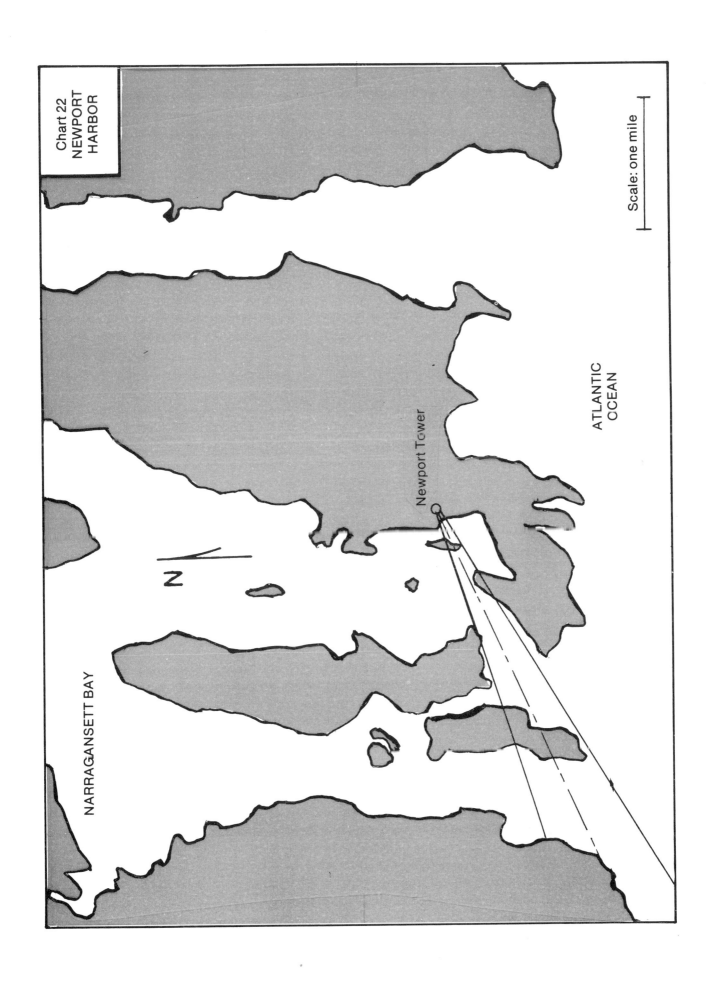

Chart 22
NEWPORT
HARBOR

Scale: one mile

ATLANTIC
OCEAN

Newport Tower

NARRAGANSETT BAY

N

Spirit Pond Mapstone. Unretouched photograph of mapstone found along the coast of Maine, having Norse runic lettering.

Photo by Malcolm Pearson.

Chart 23
STONE MAP SKETCHED
for legibility

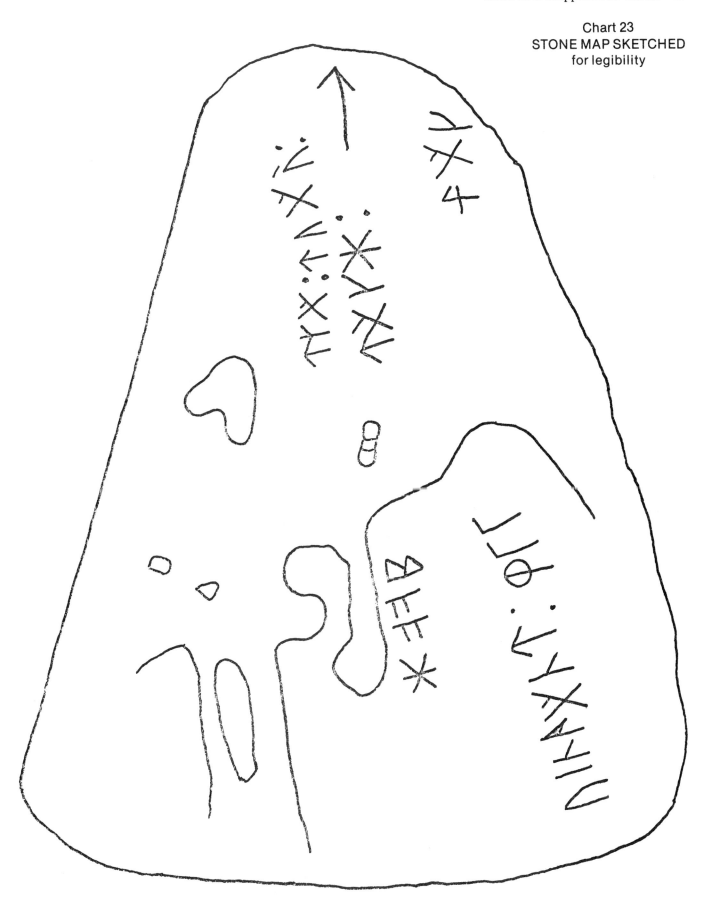

Ancient spelling, however, ranged all over the map, so to speak. The Celt on the French side of the channel is spelled "Breton," and on the English side the same race of people is spelled "Briton." Likewise the word English is spelled on the other side of the channel "Anglais." And today we see examples of this where the nation of Denmark is spelled with an "e" in our country, but they spell it with an "a" in their country. Christopher Columbus spelled his name three different ways, none of which was "Columbus."[46] It has been said that Brendan has fifteen different spellings, and the Irish themselves use Brendan and Brandon interchangeably.

One word on the Spirit Pond stone, carried from the runic letters to the Roman lettering of our language, reads "hoob," or "hoop," the letters "b" and "p" being frequently interchangeable. Most translators in turn write this in English as "hop" indicating a short "O" sound, but Magnusson and Palsson have written it as "hope" indicating the long "O" sound which is the obvious intent of the inscriber in using the double "O."

As to words, modern illustrations may help to understand the limitations in this area: "ain't" and "okay" were in widespread use in American English long before they appeared in the dictionary. (Even after "okay" appeared it had several different spellings.)

Another word, "Kilroy" was literally spread around the world by American servicemen in World War II. It was graffiti and mocked the habit of many people inscribing their own names in out of the way places. It began with "Kilroy was here" and was quickly shortened to simply "Kilroy." Every serviceman who thought he was first to discover a certain location was frequently surprised to find that "Kilroy" had already been there.

We now know of such a word in use by Norse seafarers during this exploration period which did not show up in any of the dictionaries and baffled the modern day language experts, until recently. The Sagas referred to "the woman" on board using the same Norse word as a person of the female gender; but the problem was that the listing of the persons on board in many of these instances simply did not include a woman. It was finally realized that the reference was to the socket hole in which the mast is placed—with the mast being removable while at sea. (This is discussed further elsewhere.) There is a modern day counterpart to this in the workingman's terminology: the electrician refers to connectors as being male and female.

Another word used by the explorers, directly applicable to the Vinland Sagas, is the world "Vinland" itself. Leif gave this new land this name in the year 1001 (plus or minus a year or two), and yet the earliest written Norse record in the Sagas is circa 1260 A.D.—more than two hundred years later. Simply because it was not written down does not mean it was not in use, as obviously it was.

As a consequence I would have to reject the contention of those who attempt to make decisions based on the dating of the word usage. We simply have no way of knowing, from the written record, how early words were being spoken.

The stone with which we are concerned here has no sentence structures, and therefore no grammar. No opinion as to grammar can be made under these circumstances.

In a similar sense, the script itself, or letter "styles" has been used as a guide. Two letters on these stones are suspect, but one of these appears in the earlier script called "ogham" and the other is found in later Scandinavian inscriptions.[47] The formation of letters, like the spelling of words, has been subject to considerable variations—and who knows how many more are yet to be found?

To pinpoint dates and to state unequivocal positions as to what could not have taken place is asking too much of the linguists.

The problem with the Norse is even more complex in that they took other people with them—people who spoke different languages. This is clearly seen within the limited context of the two Vinland Sagas which refer to a Scottish couple in one instance and to a German in another. Other nationalities may also have been represented as in these two instances they are cited simply because they relate to specific incidents. We know, for example, of the frequent Irish relationship with those Norse who had moved to Iceland, and then on to Greenland. Therefore "loan" words and letters might have been introduced from other languages.

Still one more problem as regards Norse runic inscriptions is that they were written by the explorer types of individuals. Sailors do not speak the language of the King's Court, and the study material is largely composed of the latter.

The pictured Spirit Pond stone is obviously a map. Several features of it struck me immediately as portraying the northern promontory of Newfoundland. Therefore a modern chart for the same area was sketched on tracing paper in order to have a direct comparison. The two are shown side by side herewith.

The island to the north of the channel is shown as a heart shape with an indention to the northwest; the same is true of Belle Isle as regards both location and having an indention to the northwest (the significance of which is that this is the landing place.) And while the stone carving is larger and somewhat exaggerated, that is not unusual even on paper maps when drawing small islands (see, for example, how Stefansson pictures the Shetland and Faeroe Islands as shown in the cartographic section). Belle Isle also loomed larger to them as it was the place where they found pasturage during that first desperate winter.

Now notice the two smaller islands between Belle Isle and the Labrador coast. The first map consulted had not shown such islands but a smaller scale nautical chart does show these small islands. That they have significance to a mariner can be found in Cartier's report where he identified them as "castles" (because of formation)—one still carries this name.

There is an object within the strait which I believe to

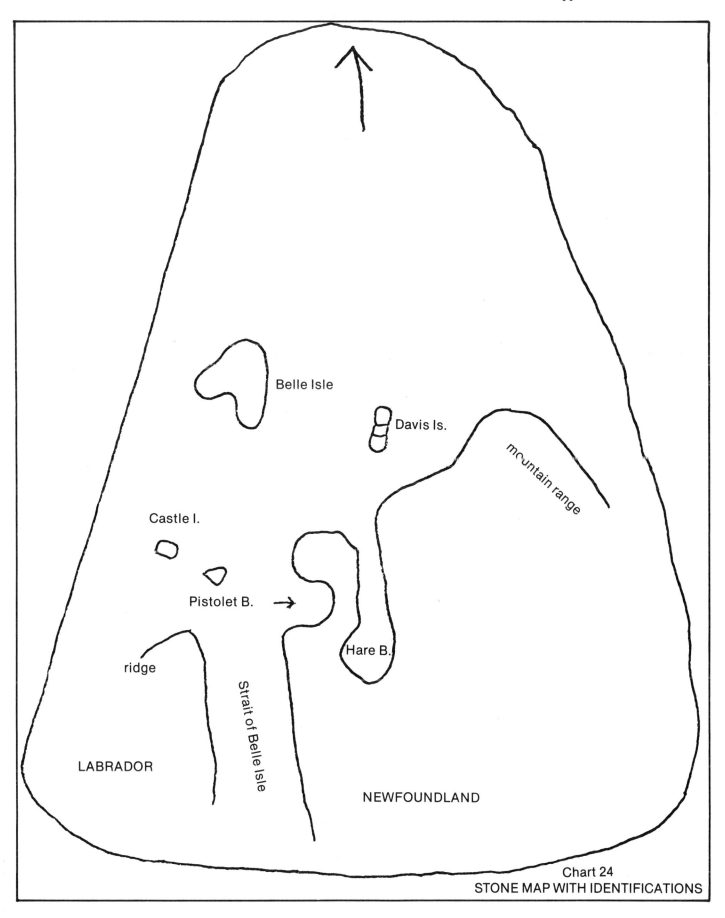

Belle Isle

Davis Is.

mountain range

Castle I.

Pistolet B. →

Hare B.

ridge

Strait of Belle Isle

LABRADOR

NEWFOUNDLAND

Chart 24
STONE MAP WITH IDENTIFICATIONS

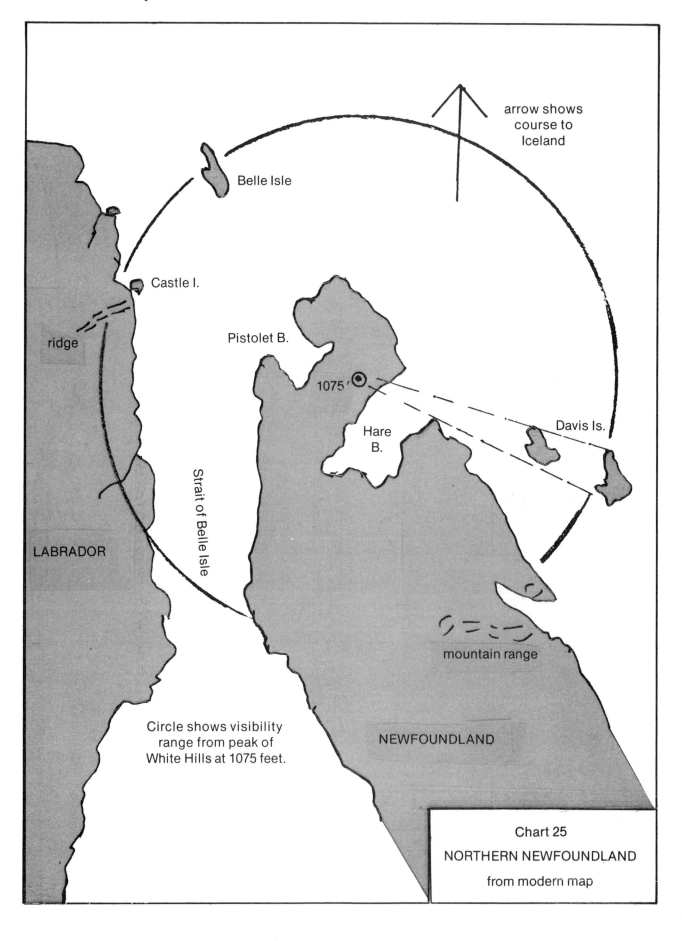

arrow shows course to Iceland

Belle Isle

Castle I.

ridge

Pistolet B.

1075'

Hare B.

Davis Is.

Strait of Belle Isle

LABRADOR

mountain range

Circle shows visibility range from peak of White Hills at 1075 feet.

NEWFOUNDLAND

Chart 25

NORTHERN NEWFOUNDLAND

from modern map

be the caricature of a whale, such as the one which saved Karlsefni's colonists from hunger following the first severe winter. More animal caricatures will be seen on the back side of this stone, each also relating to the food supply here on Newfoundland/Vinland.

Both Pistolet Bay and Cape Bauld are in their respective positions and in remarkably precise proportions. The same is true for Hare Bay, which is below and facing out toward the Atlantic. It would be difficult for a stone cutter working with a chisel to have done this more accurately.

Below this bay appears the lettering "hoop."[48] This is not the location of the Hope described by Karlsefni in the Saga and located further south at what is now called Gander Lake. One must remember that the word "hope" is generic and translates into English as a marshy or tidal lake. Hare Bay has extensive marshes around its shores.

Hare Bay, unlike Pistolet Bay, faces eastward directly on to the ocean. It is thus exposed to the daily erosion of the waves as well as to the periodic erosion of high tides and storms from the sea. It no longer is a tidal lake. But there are clues that it once was: at its mouth there are land indentions both from the north and from the south; in addition, there is a row of islands stretching almost halfway across it. Before the erosion effects of the past thousand years this land may have stretched all the way across the bay. Such a land barrier reaching to sea level would have made of Hare Bay a "hope."

The word "Hope" on the stone map, served as a warning to mariners.

Moving further southward there appear to be two or three small islands closely grouped: The nearby Gray Islands.

On the bottom left of the stone is the word "Vinlant," one of the variations of the spelling of Vinland. Next comes the date of 1011. The chronology reconstructed in chapter III shows Karlsefni's voyage as circa 1011.

Of the lettering on the right hand side, the first word translates "ten," the second word translates as two, or "ten and two" (twelve)[49]; and the next is "days." Next comes an arrow pointing off to the right. Below is the word "lag" which in a nautical sense means course or direction.[50]

On the stone both the northern promontory and the strait are parallel, which likewise shows on the modern map. On the latter this angle can be measured at 57° to true north. The arrow is not quite parallel, but slightly more to the east an additional 3°, making a total of 60° Measured on a Mercator map, in order to have a true direction, this angle would bring a ship to within sight of the mountains and glaciers of southern Iceland. The distance to southern Iceland is some 1,400 nautical miles. Twelve days' sailing with a wind from the prevailing westerlies on a northeast course at 125 miles per day average would carry the ship 1,500 miles.

Karlsefni was an Icelander, not a Greenlander. When he "returned home" he went back to Iceland. The "dead reckoning" type of plotting as regards to the direction to Iceland (which proves to be remarkably accurate) can be (and could have been) accomplished since the course and distance from Iceland to Greenland, and the course and distance from Greenland to Newfoundland were now known; it would be a simple matter of plotting the third leg of the triangle. The early Norse proved their capability in this respect in voyaging on the Iceland-Norway-Ireland-Iceland triangle.[51]

The backside of this same stone has a single word, "Milt-iaki," which translates as "pleasant land."[52] On one side is a sketch of grapes and the other side has grain stalks; below appears an Atlantic salmon, a waterfowl bird in flight, a deer stag, a squirrel, an Indian, a canoe, a bow & arrow, a stretched hide. Most of these items were cited in the Sagas. The foodstuffs were especially important to them.

Karlsefni, as shown by the courses drawn in Chapter III, did not reach down into Maine where the stone was found. The stone, however, depicts the area where they spent the first summer and winter and it could have been made at that time. It conforms with the date shown on it.

It is a location map. Its purpose was likely for the other colonists to follow. In the year 1011 Karlsefni still had hopes of founding a permanent settlement.

Why a stone map? The answer is simple: they sailed in open boats and the stone would not only be preserved, it could also be read in any kind of weather.

Note that the name "Vinland" is not placed on the northern tip, nor nearby the bay adjoining which was the river and lake location of Leif's cabins. Instead, it appears, in the lower left hand corner of the map with the land lines on both of the sides continuing, but incomplete—the standard mapmaker's indication of land continuing. For a location map only the upper area was needed as this is the part encountered in the landfall approach previously discussed.

The use of the term "Vinland" in this manner further verifies the authenticity of the map. Heretofore it had not been realized that the word referred to Newfoundland, as a whole. Conjecture ran from Baffin Island to Carolina, with even those favoring Newfoundland disagreeing as to its location on the island rather than recognizing it was the entire land mass.

The contents of the map drawings reflect Karlsefni's experiences: the whale in Straumfjord, the prominence of Belle Isle. The backside is something of a promotion poster, showing the many food items obtainable, and the native Amerindian as directly connected with the trading of pelts. Considering the work time element involved and explained below, it is likely that this reverse side is a later addition.

From internal evidence on the map itself it is possible to locate the vantage point from which the map was drawn: the high ground which rises to 1,075 feet above sea level on the north side of Hare Bay (indicated on the map shown here). This is the highest land nearby Leif's cabins, where

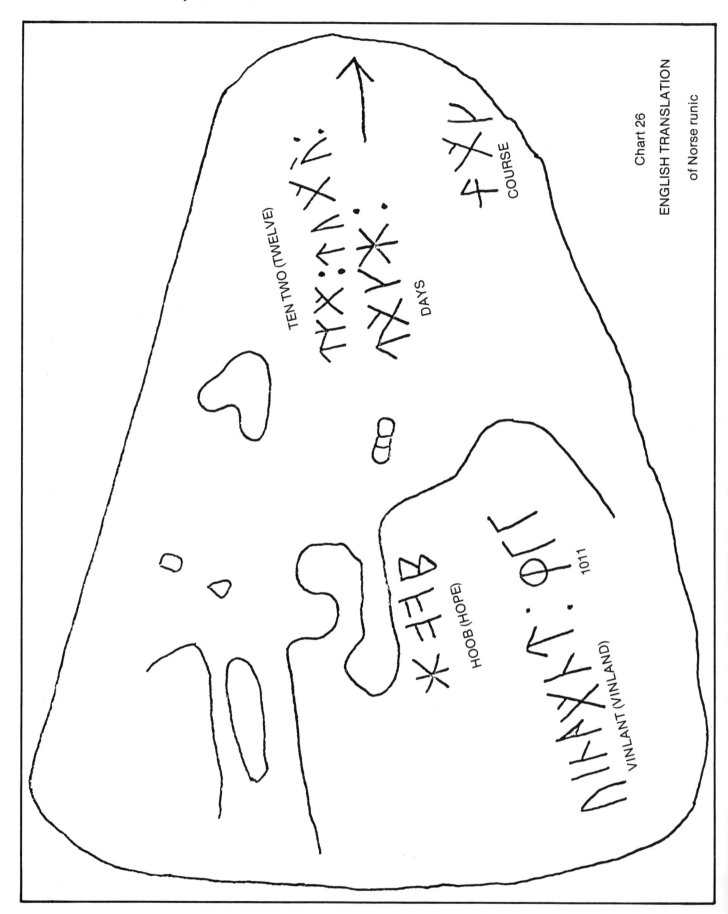

TEN TWO (TWELVE)

DAYS

COURSE

HOOB (HOPE)

VINLANT (VINLAND)

1011

Chart 26
ENGLISH TRANSLATION
of Norse runic

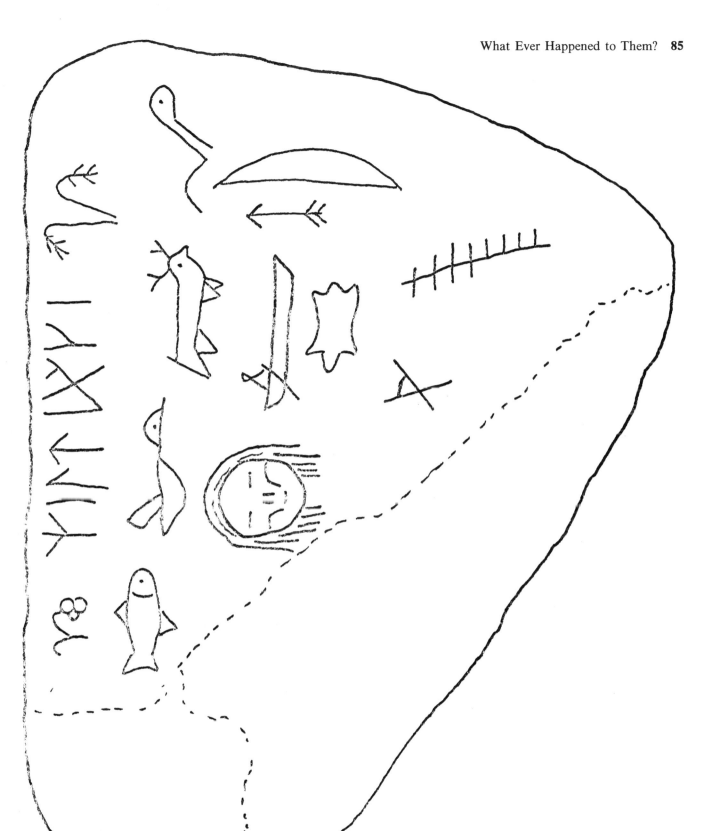

Reverse of Mapstone, which helped author identify the maker of the frontside.   Karlsefni promoted the colonization of Vinland, and this is a promotion piece showing the plentiful foodstuffs—and the Indian as a source of trade.

A tracing by Donal Buchanan of Malcolm Pearson's photograph.

Coat of Arms, Newfoundland. Granted in 1637, note the resemblance between the Indians pictured here and the one on the mapstone: straight hair, slotted eyes, broad cheekbones.

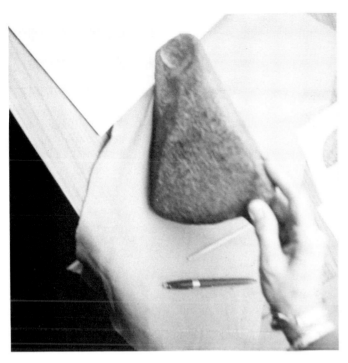

Mapstone, hand held, to illustrate size.

Photo by author.

Karlsefni was first located and the logical point from which to view and map the northern promontory.

From this altitude can be seen all of the physical features illustrated on the map. The White Hills, as these mountains are called, are barren on their upper level and consequently have unobstructed views. There are four elements of the stone map which are peculiar to and could only have been made by a mapmaker drawing from this location:

1. Both the North Grey Island and South Grey Island are visible from this point, with one being behind the other and they thus appear to be connected as the map shows them—yet the mapmaker recognized that one was beyond the other. In the distance we see hills which are further out as a different shade of coloring from those closer to us.
2. The shoreline of Labrador from its southeast corner veers back too sharply to the northwest. This is caused by the viewer seeing the ridge rather than the far coastline, from this point on the White Hills.
3. The entire physical scope of the map is the same as the visibility range of the observer on the hill.
4. Even the appearance of the land mass turning back west below the Grey Islands is attributable to a sighting from the White Hills. The peaks to the south are located in such a pattern.

This mapstone also has on it information which was peculiar to Karlsefni's experience:

1. The already mentioned location of the indention on Belle Isle, which is not visible from the mapmaker's location but was already known.
2. The drawing of Belle Isle is larger than the Grey Islands, even though their sizes are about the same, but the former had already been visited.
3. The Grey Islands are not separated inasmuch as Karlsefni in the year 1011 had not yet made his trip south and they therefore had not sailed past them to ascertain the separation.
4. The use of the word "Hope" on Hare Bay. Although both Leif and Thorvald had entered a tidal lake, neither used this term. Karlsefni, familiar with it being used for a similar bay nearby his home in Iceland, uses it here.[48]
5. The whale in the Strait of Belle Isle which was peculiar to Karlsefni's experience within this group of voyages;
6. Hare Bay is shown as going much further inland to the west than it does today, just as would be expected as the western end is now a swampy area and the geologists tell us that this land has since risen.

The weight of the evidence is that this is a map drawn by Karlsefni, or under his direction, in the year 1011 as shown on the face thereof. It is the earliest known map of any part of America which can be authenticated

L'Anse Aux Meadows

The most famous of the Norse sites, and the most widely accepted, is located at a remote fishing village on northern Newfoundland now called L'Anse Aux Meadows. Among those accepting it as authentic are archeologists Henry Collins of the Smithsonian Institute and Junius Bird of the American Museum of Natural History. Their endorsement, it must be noted, was limited to identifying it as a Norse inhabitation and not as Leif's houses site.[53]

In 1980 it was officially proclaimed a World Heritage Site by the United Nations. Helge and his wife Anne Stine Ingstad were present for the ceremony and honors.

While L'Anse Aux Meadows cannot be the site of Leif's houses, it can account for the visit received by Karlsefni of local natives. Leif had limited his crew to explorations which could be completed within one day and therefore the L'Anse Aux Meadows site would have been beyond the range of their scouts from Pistolet Bay, traveling over land. It is not far as the crow flies, but it is separated by an inlet. Karlsefni, on the other hand, had a larger population which must have (from necessity when seeking food) ranged wider and therefore been more noticeable to the people at L'Anse Aux Meadows. While it cannot be said for certain that these were the same people who came to Karlsefni's village, it can be stated that the physical conditions, both as regards time and geography, accord with the historical record.

Other

In 1973 a study done by Bruce J. Bourque, Research Associate of the Maine State Museum, was published dealing with aborginal settlements along that coast. The findings showed a change had taken place in the seasonal activities of the natives: whereas earlier for many centuries it had been a coastal economy, it shifted to a settlement system in which March through May were spent trapping, hunting, and fishing in the interior with marine exploration coming later during the warmer months of the year. The author, while unable to pinpoint the exact time of the changeover, postulates that the cause could have been the Norse trading for furs with the Maine Indians.[54] This would be in keeping with the evidence from the European side that furs of North American land animals were being brought into the Old World as common trade items.

Another navigational type of evidence was found: mooring holes. These are holes made in stone boulders beside rivers and bays which are used to hold an anchor pin attached to a rope holding the ship. With the land forested, why did they not tie the rope to a tree instead of going to all of the trouble of digging out a hole in a stone? The answer is simple: the pin could be lifted out or flipped out in a fraction of a second in case of attack by hostiles.

Fredrick J. Pohl, who has done much research on the Norse voyaging, points out in his book *The Lost Discovery* that the mooring holes found over a wide area of present day New England are of the Norse type. That is they are cut in a rounded triangular fashion rather than the round hole fashion in common use elsewhere.

Various types of artifacts have been found: not only the stone tower at Newport, Rhode Island, and the runic carvings such as the stone map at Spirit Pond, Maine; but also statuary in the form of a stone head with distinct Norse features found on Ungava Bay in upper Quebec (among stone cairns and shelters which Canadian archeologist Thomas E. Lee also believes to be Norse), and a Norse penny, struck in Norway during the period 1065 to 1080 A.D. The latter, found in an Indian ruin on the coast of Maine in 1961, has only been recently identified and declared authentic.

As we go forward we are learning more about the past.[55]

Ethnological Evidence

While in Iceland doing research, my wife and I had the fortunate experience of meeting a Danish couple who were both orthopedic surgeons there for a conference in their field. Earlier the lady surgeon had been given a one-year

Norse Penny from the 11th Century. Obverse and reverse sides. We are fortunate in having these pictures as the coin has visibly deteriorated since having been found in a burial mound in Maine.

Photo courtesy Maine State Museum.

assignment by the nation of Denmark to care for the needs of the people in Greenland within her field of specialization. Over dinner one evening she recounted one of the surprising experiences she had while there.

Shortly after arrival she addressed one of the local people in Danish assuming that the young lady was one of the many Danes living in Greenland. She was tall, fine featured, blue eyed, blond, and had the appearance of a fellow country-man. Instead, the girl answered back in the Greenlandic dialect of the Eskimo language. She was an Eskimo. In view of the long time of the association between the Norsemen and the Eskimos while the original colonies were in existance, as well as the relatively long period of time and co-existance there between the Danes and the Eskimos since the reestab-lishment of the European outpost, it would be impossible to tell whether the genes in the "Eskimo" woman were of recent integration or go back perhaps for centuries. It would not be the only encounter of this type for the lady doctor.

Vilhjalmur Steffansson, the famous artic explorer, had a similar encounter with a whole tribe of Eskimos while on an extended stay in the far North. Steffansson, incidentally, is a direct decendent of Karlsefni and Gudrid. This line of decent comes through their first son Snorri, who was born in Vinland/Newfoundland, before the family returned to Iceland. Steffansson himself was born of parents who had immigrated to Manitoba, Canada from Iceland in the 1800's. He attended the Universities of North Dakota, Iowa, and Harvard, studying anthropology.

Subsequently he spent ten winters and seven summers in the far North, where he learned to speak Eskimo, and gathered much of our present day knowledge of the Arctic. During World War II, he was the advisor to our Armed Forces for arctic survival kits and manuals supplied to those of us for whom it was necessary to travel in these areas.

Steffansson, during his travels in the North, had found a tribe of Eskimos on Victoria Island, many of whom had a European appearance. Victoria is far to the west of the early Norse Western Settlement on Greenland and beyond Baffin Island, as well as Hudson Bay. Its inaccessibility, even today makes it practically unknown.

The Eskimos to the south described them to Steffansson as "people who look very much as I did, having reddish beards and some of them, blue eyes."

Steffansson says "these people were, as we had been told, the most widely traveled of all the Eskimos. They certainly were the most unusual in appearance. Natkusiak (his travel-ing Eskimo companion) and I agreed that among them there was a greater percentage of individuals who looked like Europeans than we had found elsewhere." And, at this time, they were not in direct contact with Europeans.

In his reports the explorer further states that they were "a physiognomy in coloring quite unlike other Eskimos" and that "most of whom had never seen a white man." Vil-hjalmur Steffansson however in the true scientist dedication to accuracy added, "There is no reason for insisting now or ever that the 'blond Eskimos' of Victoria Island are de-scended from the Scandinavian colonists of Greenland, but looking at it historically or geographically there is no reason why they might not be."

Steffansson is likewise meticulous in not claiming to have "discovered" these people, pointing out that others did so prior to his contact in 1910: Dr. John Rea, an Englishman in a Royal Geographical report, re an expedition on behalf of the Hudson Bay Company; who in turn was preceded by John Franklin in 1824, and Thomas Hudson in 1837.

There are even earlier historical records: DeQuincit Poin-cy's *Historie Neturelle & Morale Des Iels Antilles de l'Ameri-que,* published in Rotterdam in 1658, had a captain of a vessel which had visited Davis Strait describing the natives on its shore (northern Labrador/Markland): As regards the inhabitants, our travelers report having seen two kinds who live together on the most friendly terms. Of these, one kind is described as "very tall, well built, of rather fair complexion . . . the other very much smaller, have an olive complexion, and tolerably well proportioned except that their legs are short and thick."

In still one more instance the Corte Real brothers, just after 1500, saw natives in Labrador (Markland) who looked to them fairer and more European like than the ordinary inhabitants of the Americas.[56]

Another American, Arlington Mallery, became interested in another group of "white natives" and followed Steffans-son's example of going to live with them in order to learn their language and customs and whatever was possible of their histories and traditions.

Mallery was an engineer working on the first steel arch bridge which he had designed and his company was building in Canada when he was fascinated in watching the iron workers climb the skeleton frame work. As he says, "It was not their skill that had caught my attention, it was their physical appearance. They looked much like the usual gang of iron workers. They had the same weather-beaten skin and essentially the same build, except that they were a little taller. The interesting thing about the group as a whole was that they all seemed to be Swedes or Norwegians." He then asked his foreman where he had found the group.

The response was, "Everyone of these men carries a card from Uncle Sam showing that he is a full-blooded Indian, a Mohawk from the St. Regis reservation in Northern New York. They all belong to a bridgeman union which takes in only registered Iroquois Indians." (The Mohawks are one of the tribes in the Iroquois confederation.)[57]

At the time, Mallery recalled only thinking oddly that these "Indians" could easily pass as the descendents of the legendary Vikings. But the seed had been planted and he began making inquiry into the question both from the Ameri-can side and Icelandic records of the Sagas. Having found further clues that are shown in some of the examples of the history section of this book, Mallery made the decision to go and live with the Iroquois to learn more about them.

Initially he found only a few of the old Norse words in the Iroquois languages, but they were there and Mallery reminded himself that the Norsemen had overrun such areas as the Normandy Peninsula in France, but subsequently adopted the French language; when these Norse people as (Normans) moved on over into England, they also conquered but again adapted the local language, English. Only a few Norse words were brought in and are now to be found as remnants, just as with the Iroquois.[58]

Here are some of the examples which Mallery has listed (more in his book):

English	Norse	Iroquoian
and	ok	ok
day	stunda	unda
devil	loki	loki
dish	ker	kerat
eat	ata	ate
girl	ekka	eksaa
god	njord	niyoh
relate	gatu	gata
she	sa	eksa
the	ina	na
wait	hara	kerhare
woman	kwenna	ishkwen

He found from their oral history the Iroquois did not report that they came from the northwest, the direction of the Siberian-Alaskan land bridge as has been speculated by non-Indian historians, but instead insisted that they themselves came from the north and northeast.[59] This is, of course, the direction of Vinland/Newfoundland, Markland/Labrador, and Greenland.

They were now living in the St. Lawrence Valley, the same area which Thorvald's crew had originally explored.

Mallery points out that the Iroquois tribes to the west have a darker skin. Also the Sieur de Robervel, the first governor general of New France, described the Iroquois in 1542 as "they are a people of goodly stature and well made; they are very white, but they are all naked and if they were appareled as the French are, they would be as white and as fair, but they paint themselves for fear of heat and sunburning."[60]

Mallery found that in the decorative arts they were using the Norsemen's chevron as well as the triad; symbol of the gods in ancient Scandinavia; in Iroquois law, the Norse system of compensation for injury or death had been used; in housing, the Iroquois were using the same style and construction as the Norse long house; even their fortifications were similar in structure to those found earlier in northern Europe.[61]

The southern side of the St. Lawrence Valley was included in the original maps showing Norumbega. Later, the French claimed this as "part of New France" and "Norumbega" was relegated only to that part lying to the south and east of the Appalachians, which is now called New England.

Here on the east coast of what is now called Narragansett Bay, the explorer Giovanni da Verrazzano in the year 1524 found natives who, he said, "They excel us in size; they are of bronze color, some inclining more to whiteness, others to tawny color; the face sharply cut . . ."[62] Verrazzano remained here only 15 days, hoping to have established an on-going friendship for the future.

Later, Roger Williams, the Pilgrim who founded Rhode Island, spent more time with these "Indians" and thus had more opportunity to observe their physical features. He described them as "tawnie, by the sun and their annointings, yet they are born white." This particular tribe occupied the specific area which Mercator had shown on his map in smaller type as Norumbega, with the larger area also named Norumbega in larger type.

Algonquin, like Iroquois, is a name applied to a number of tribes. These, too, were peoples occupying much of the northeastern United States at the beginning of our Colonial Period.

The Algonquin played a game which they taught latter-day Americans and which we now call LaCrosse. It is identical in its essential features to the old Norse game of Knattleikr, using paired opponents whose interactions may not be interfered with by other players—so unique as to rule out the likelihood of coincidence in the genesis of the game.[63]

The Algonquin, like the Iroquois, have Norse loan words in their language. Reider T. Sherwin includes these in his study titled *The Viking and the Red Man*.[64]

The Beothucks are the natives of Newfoundland at the time of arrival of the Europeans during the "Colonial Period." They are generally described as "indians" but they did not look like the Amerindian. Instead of a brown skin they had a white skin; instead of high cheek bones and broad features, they had the fine lines of Caucasians. In fact, when the English and Portugese explorers took captives back home and dressed them as Europeans they were described in both cases as being indistinguishable from Europeans.

The Frenchman Cartier, described the Beothucks: "There are people on this coast whose bodies are fairly well formed, but they are wild and savage folk. They wear their hair tied up on the top of their heads like a hand full of twisted hay . . . they paint themselves with certain tan colors. They have canoes of birch bark in which they go about, and from which they catch many seals. Since seeing them I have been informed that their home is not at this place but that they come from warmer countries to catch these seals . . ."[65]

Cartier was on the north coast of the Gulf of St. Lawrence (Quebec and Southern Labrador). His informer was correct, the Beothucks lived south of here in Newfoundland, and at that time, on Cape Breton Island. The tan color of paint to which he refers is the red ochre when it is dried. And the hay colored hair indicates a blond or brownette—not the black hair of the Amerindian.

Their arrival in the Newfoundland area is usually described as "mysterious" and/or "of unknown origin"; the time as "? AD." The Irish knew of the land beyond the Ocean Sea at the time of Brendan the Navigator (564 A.D.) when it was already known to his predecessors. The Norse knew of the Irish visits here at the time of the Eric family voyages (1001 to 1015 A.D.); and the Icelandic histories record an incident of contact with the Irish in these lands.

The Norse followed the Celtic/Irish peoples into the Hebrides, the Shetlands, the Faeroes, and Iceland. And we now know through blood types and other evidence that the people of Iceland are actually a mixture of Irish and Norse, although their language and history is that of the Norse, who dominated.

We now go back to Chapter I and recall that the Carbon 14 dates at the L'Anse Aux Meadows site range all the way back to 640 A.D. There are four more of these in the 700's, five more in the 800's and still one more in the 900's. The Irish cultural pattern was similar to that of the Norse, and it must be viewed as a possibility at least that these earlier European type settlements were Irish/Celtic. If so, might the Beothucks be a mixture of the Celtic and Norse peoples just as in Iceland?

This in turn leads to another fascinating question: Were they responsible for the introduction of the bow and arrow to the American Indian? According to archeologist Stuart Struever "Most people when they think of Amerindians, assume they always used bows and arrows. Actually, during most of prehistory in North America the aborigines used spears, tipped with stone projectile points. It was not until about AD 800 that they began using bows and arrows."[66]

And along with this is the equally intriguing question: Did the Irish/Celtic and/or the Norse introduce the canoe to the American Indian? The canoe of which we are speaking is not the dugout type found in the Caribbean, but rather the one which is frequently called "a birch-bark canoe" even though it was found to be skin covered in early instances in New England. The design of the canoe is almost identical to that of the smaller type of currachs, still in use in Ireland, and previously known to both the Irish and the Norse. It is double ended (that is pointed at both ends), it employs the displacement principle with a thin outer shell (of whatever material), braced by an internal structure of light wood framing. In the *Navigatio Sancti Brendani*[67] it is described as "a very light-weight, small vessel, ribbed and columned from the wood which is the custom in those regions, and they covered it with cow hides." Whether cow hides, deer, or moose skins[68] or birch bark or the modern day aluminum, the canoe is still the same invention. As Thor Heyerdahl

points out in his new book *Early Man and the Ocean,* the design of a vessel which would transport people and cargo across the water surfaces was not an easy one, nor did it, in Heyerdahl's opinion and reasoning, develop out of the dugout canoe.

CHRONOLOGY OF EARLY IRISH/NORSE REPORTS

Circa

564–5 AD	Brendan's voyage, following other Irishmen, to "The Land Promised the Saints."
640±30	Earliest Carbon 14 date at European type settlement, L'Anse Aux Meadows, Newfoundland.
725 & earlier	Irish were in the Faeroes, according to Dicuil, Irish scholar at the Court of Charlemagne
795	Clerics report their Iceland living experience to Dicuil.
825	Dicuil writes that the earth is spherical and the extremities are uninhabitable.
860	Norse discover Iceland
900+	Ari Marsson is storm driven to "Greater Ireland," is baptized there, later seen and reported by other Icelanders.
1014	Native boys, captured by Karlsefni, refer to the country across from their own land, which the Norse believe to be Greater Ireland.
1029	Gudlief Gudlaugson, Icelandic merchant driven by a storm southwestward, finds Bjorn Asbrandson, another Icelander, living among Irish speaking peoples.

The Beothucks used their canoes even out on the open waters of the Strait of Belle Isle and up the Atlantic coast of Labrador.

If they were originally Europeans, one may ask why they did not stay in touch with Europe? Why should they have stayed in touch? Europe offered taxations from foreign kings, taxation from the church, serfdom in the fields, conscription in the armies, piracy on the seas, and the black plague.

The Beothucks painted their persons with red ochre. This is a pigment picked up through the local clay, which when mixed with water becomes a mud and easily applicable. Not originally understood, it is now believed that this served the purpose of an insect repellent and accordingly may have

Mary March, one of the last known survivors of the people called Beothucks. This painting, by Henrietta, Lady Hamilton, wife of the Governor of Newfoundland is the only known one made from real life. The original is in the Public Archives of Canada at Ottawa.

Photo courtesy Public Archives of Canada, (C-87698).

been mixed with a natural chemical unknown to us. As such, they were generations ahead of their time, and yet well adapted to their locale. Newfoundland, like Ireland, has no snakes. But this also means that they have a sizable insect population in the summertime and even the modern day tourist brochures warn against this. Bring repellent. Unfortunately for the Beothucks, it made them "look different."

On arrival of the English and Frence during the Colonial Period, they found the local people to be formidable adversaries for control of the land and fiercely independent. Thus, they were "enemies" and systematically killed off with firearms.

Little has been known about them as they were literally "not on speaking terms" with the new arrivals. Even when the English policy changed over to intended peaceful co-existance they were unable to communicate because of the fears the natives then held. One person who has made a study of the Beothuck and personally spent years collecting artifacts from their occupation sites is Don Locke.[69] A reconstructed Beothuck village is now located in the Province of Newfoundland, nearby the city of Grand Falls.

The solid evidence of their culture can be found in the physical remains left behind at their living sites. While many of their houses were "wigwams" of the Amerindian style with poles in a conical shape, other buildings were of the post and beam construction in the European fashion. The pieces were joined with the red root, which is the same methodology used in the reconstruction of the Norse sites at L'Anse Aux Meadows. Some of these Beothuck buildings were long houses, the European style.

The Beothucks built drying racks for food in the European fashion, had smoke houses for curing food in the European fashion, and stored food in pits in the European fashion.

They used iron metals in making arrow heads, spears, knives, and harpoons. This has been attributed to their stealing iron implements from the later European colonizers and converting them into their own items. One must ask, however, if they were stealing why did they not steal guns; and if they learned the technology of metalsmithing (for conversion) from these later Europeans why they did not learn the technology of gunsmithing from them? At the L'Anse Aux Meadows site is a metalsmithy which was operating there in prior centuries, utilizing local pig iron deposits, and capable of making the metal arrow heads and other weapons. The bow and arrow was a weapon known to the old world at least as far back as Biblical times, but unknown to the new world until about 800 A.D. This date, it will be noted, overlaps the occupation dates found at the L'Anse Aux Meadows site.

A final clue as to the origins of the Beothuck is found in the "Sauna." This is a distinct Norse cultural invention and used only in the Scandinavian countries up until recent times.

It was ironic that the young lady guide showing us through the Beothuck village described the Sauna practice, seemingly unaware that it was a Norse practice also. But, then again, most of us have been unaware of the Beothucks.

The people occupying the L'Anse Aux Meadows site in the 11th century also had a Sauna, and its remains can still be found there.

Following is a statement furnished by the Director of the Mary March Museum, Mr. Glenn Stroud.

THE STORY OF MARY MARCH

By the early 1800's the number of Beothuck Indians, the original inhabitants of Newfoundland, had diminished considerably from their population high of several thousand. During that period the Governor offered a reward of fifty pounds for the capture of a Beothuck Indian alive. The intention was to teach a captured Indian English and allow him to return to his people so that through him a peaceful relationship could be established between the Beothuck and English peoples and consequently the tribe saved from imminent extinction.

In 1819 Governor Charles Hamilton authorized an expedition of settlers led by John Peyton Jr., a Twillingate merchant, to approach the Indians to recover some items which had been stolen and if possible, to capture and return with a Beothuck.

The expedition travelled along the Exploits River from Notre Dame Bay. Their destination was Red Indian Lake the winter habitation site of the Indian tribe. The expedition took five days to travel the sixty miles and reported . . .

On the morning of March 5, 1819 they came across an encampment of three wigwams on the north eastern part of the lake. Surprised by the appearance of the expedition the Indians fled into the nearby forest. Peyton gave chase to an Indian woman who soon became exhausted and surrendered to him. As he approached, the woman opened her caribou hide tunic and exposed her breasts apparently to show that she was a woman and to request mercy.

The woman's name was Demasduit but she was soon renamed by the English settlers, with the month of her capture in mind as Mary March. She was about twenty three years old at the time of her capture and was later described as being ". . . tall with a rather stout body, delicate arms and beautifully formed hands and feet. Her complexion was a light copper colour and her hair black."

Although most of the Indians had run off when the expedition approached, one known as Nonsbawsut, the husband of the captured woman and chief of the tribe returned when he saw that his wife was unable to escape.

The settlers later reported that he stood approximately six feet seven inches tall and had a full beard. He stood about ten yards from his wife and her captors and delivered a long oration in the Beothuck language lasting about ten minutes. As it was, neither side in the confrontation spoke the other's language and neither party could explain its actions. Peyton was unable to explain that his intention was to establish peace between the two peoples. Lack of communication and the way in which the expedition behaved was sufficient proof to the Indians that their motives were unfriendly.

When his oration had no effect upon the expedition members, Nonsbawsut moved in closer and attempted to remove their hands from his wife's arms. Her captors opposed and her husband became enraged. He drew from beneath his cossack an axe and waved it in the air. Mary March's captors continued to restrain her and started to move her towards the lakeshore. This infuriated the husband further and he rushed towards them. In the ensuing commotion he was stabbed in the back and shot several times by Peyton's men. He succumbed to his injuries.

Mary March journeyed with the expedition down river and managed to escape once but was quickly recaptured. She spent several months in Twillingate in the care of a Reverend Leigh, an Episcopal Missionary. Later that same year, she was taken to St. John's where she became a popular figure. While there a portrait of her, described as ". . . a good likeness" was painted by Lady Hamilton, the wife of the Governor. This is the only known portrait of a Beothuck painted from life and is now in the collection of the Public Archives of Canada, Ottawa. Later, during the same year, it was ascertained that she had a young child that was left behind at the time of her capture. With that in mind and the fact that she had learned some of the English language efforts were made to restore her to her people and hopefully, through her open communications with them. Captain Buchan of the vessel "Grasshopper" was despatched late in 1819 to the Bay of Exploits with the woman and with orders to return her to the place of her capture. Before Mary March could be reunited with her people she died of tuberculosis on board ship near Botwood on January 8, 1820. The body was placed in a coffin along with such trinkets as she had collected during the previous year. The coffin was taken up the river to Red Indian Lake and left where her people would find it. It was subsequently found by them and she was buried next to her husband.

Within four years of the capture of Mary March only one known member of the Beothuck tribe, Shawnawdithit, remained alive. Within ten years of the incident, 1829, she also succumbed to tuberculosis and the tribe was extinct.

The story of Mary March is a tragic one. She was remembered not for what she did but for what was done to her. Her story and particularly the incidents at the time of her capture encapsulated the host of misunderstandings and lack of communication on both sides which characterized the relations between the settlers and the Beothuck Indians. What happened here is not unique and in fact, is often found in varying degrees when two cultures meet. The story of Mary March is a tragic one—but not one which should be ignored or allowed to be forgotten.

SUGGESTED READING:

Howley, J.P. *The Beothucks or Red Indians The Aboriginal Inhabitants of Newfoundland.* Toronto, Coles Publishing Co. Ltd., 1974.

Rowe, Frederick W. *Extinction. The Beothuks of Newfoundland.* Scarborough, Ontario. McGraw Hill Ryerson Ltd, 1977.

Marshall, Ingeborg. *The Red Ochre People.* Vancouver, J.J. Douglas Ltd., 1977

While the above describes Mary March as having "a light copper colour" complexion, a study done by Ingeborg Marshall, graduate student, Department of Anthropology and Archeology, Memorial University of Newfoundland, and published in the Newfoundland Quarterly is more illuminating. It states "Comtemporaries describe Mary March as a young woman, about 23 years of age, of a gentle and interesting disposition, as very active, tall, with a stout body and small and delicate limbs. Her complexion initially a light copper colour, became *nearly as fair as Europeans*' after a course of washing and absence from smoke." (The Beothucks' buildings, like the early European buildings, had no chimneys, but only an open hole in the roof to let out smoke.)

The use of the word "tunic" to describe her upper garment at the time of capture recalls that the Saga used the same word to describe a native woman's style of dress.

And Mary's husband's garment is described as a "cassock," a long coat style known in Europe, and unlike the jackets of the Amerindians.

One thing which must be borne in mind in the study of Norse exploration in America is that here, unlike elsewhere, they did not dominate. Whatever advantages they had with their iron swords was not enough to offset the numerical advantage of the Amerindian. Not until Columbus came along with a small army equipped with guns did the Europeans begin to dominate in racial stock and culture.

The Norse assimilation into the Amerindian tribal groups becomes more understandable when we understand the nature of the early Norse themselves, as well as their counterparts, the Amerindians.

First of all the Norse were similar to the Amerindian in being primarily hunters and fishermen. Their agriculture was mostly animal husbandry. Today, in the Faeroes and

Iceland and many parts of Norway this is still the case.

Even the animal husbandry lent itself to the changeover in culture. Originally the Europeans practiced what we were to later call "open range" here in America. Barbed wire fences were not invented until the 1800's. Prior to this cattle and other livestock roamed freely and it was a problem even up into this century when paved roads and high-speed highways forced a change in the laws in favor of the motorists.

The native Indian, for his part, practiced a somewhat similar animal husbandry: he cleared forests so that there would be grazing ground for the deer. Thus when Eric, Karlsefni, and the others began arriving and cutting timber, they were performing a service to the natives who were already there.

Many men, even within the recorded historical periods, have shown a preference for hunting and fishing over the humdrum labors of farming and animal husbandry. While true today, it was even more so in those time periods when people lived in harsher environments and did not enjoy the comforts of modern day life.

During the 1700's and 1800's here in America this preference for the native way of life appeared so frequently that a term developed to describe it: "gone native."

This preference was eloquently expressed by one of the Indian chiefs in the Colonial Period. The Virginia colonists had suggested to representatives of the Iroquois Indian Nations that they might send some of their young braves to the college of William and Mary.

The response of the Onondago chief, Canastego, was: "But you, who are wise, must know that different Nations have different conceptions of things; and you will therefore not take it amiss, if our ideas of this kind of education happen not to be the same with yours. We have had some experience of it; several of our young people were formerly brought up at the Colleges of the Northern Provinces; they were instructed in all your sciences; but, when they came back to us, they were bad runners, ignorant of every means of living in the woods, unable to bear either cold or hunger, knew neither how to build a cabin, take a deer, or kill an enemy, spoke our language imperfectly, were therefore neither fit for hunters, warriors, nor counselors; they were totally good for nothing.

"We are however not the less obliged by your kind offer, tho' we decline accepting it; and, to show our grateful sense of it, if the gentlemen of Virginia will send us a dozen of their sons, we will take care of their education, instruct them in all we know, and make men of them."

VII

Human Relations Lessons

Accounts of the five voyages to Vinland contained within the Sagas, are brief, but nonetheless cover a wide range of actions following human emotions and their consequences. First there is the obvious love for adventure in youth. Eric as a young man ventures out to Greenland, but in later years is reluctant to go forward to Vinland. His son Leif, then the young man, carries forward this mission.

On return, Leif ran the risk of picking up a stranded crew. (They may have been pirates and Leif recognized the possible problem by keeping his ship as close to the wind as possible which would have allowed them a quick turn and get away if necessary.) Not only did he do this but he took the people on board home with him and gave them a home in his home for the winter, sharing his provisions. It was necessary to thus be provided in order to live through the winter, and in the Norse records there are frequent instances of this kind of charity being shown to their fellow man.

Another instance involves Tyrkir, a German serf who had helped to raise Leif and had been taken along on his voyage. (The Norse during this period enslaved both Germans and Irish to use as their servants). But when Tyrkir strayed from the others in a land exploration party, Leif became quite upset and on finding him calls him "foster father." Thus as so often has happened throughout recorded history slaves have won over their masters through love.

Freydis, the daughter of Eric, had the courage to simulate her brothers in an expedition to Vinland. But she also had the greed to cause this otherwise successful expedition to culminate in tragedy and a lifetime of sorrow. Here's how it happened, as described by the Saga:

When winter set in, the brothers, Helgi and Finnbogi, suggested that they should start holding games and other entertainments. This was done for a while until trouble broke out and ill feeling arose among the two parties. The games were abandoned and all visiting between the houses ceased; and this state of affairs continued for most of the winter.

One night Freydis slipped out to go and visit with the brothers, unbeknownst to her husband. She asked Finnbogi to step out and talk with her.

"How are you getting along?" she asked.

"I like this good country," he replied, "but I dislike the ill feeling that has arisen between us because I can see no reason for it."

"You are right," she said, "and I feel the same about it as you do. But the reason that I came to see you is that I want to exchange ships with you and your brother for your ship is larger than mine and I want to go away from here."

"I shall agree to that," he said, "if that will make you happy."

Freydis returned to her cabin and her bed, but her feet were cold which awoke her husband who wanted to know why.

She answered with great indignation, "I went over to see the brothers to offer to buy their ship, because I want a larger one; and this made them so angry that they struck me and handled me very roughly. But you, you wretch, would never avenge even my humiliation or your own. I realize now how far I am away from my home in Greenland! Unless you avenge this, I am going to divorce you."

He could bear her taunts no longer and told his men to get up at once and take their weapons. They did so and went straight over to the brothers' house; they broke in while all of the men were asleep, seized them and tied them up, and dragged them outside one by one. Freydis had each of them put to death as soon as he came out.

All the men were killed in this way, and soon only the women were left; but no one was willing to kill them.

Freydis said, "Give me an ax."

This was done; and she herself killed the women, all five of them.

Freydis now had both ships loaded "with all the produce they could get and the ship could carry." She warned her crew that on return to Greenland "I shall have anyone killed who breathes a word about what has happened. Our story will be that these people stayed on here when we left."

When they returned to Greenland, as the Saga says

She loaded her companions with money for she wanted them to keep her crimes secret; and then she settled down on the farm.

But her companions were not all discrete enough to say nothing about these evil crimes and prevent them from becoming known. Eventually the word reached the ears of her brother Leif, who thought it a hideous story. He seized three of Freydis's men and tortured them into revealing everything that had happened; their stories tallied exactly.

"I do not have the heart," said Leif, "to punish my sister Freydis as she deserves. But I prophesy that she will never prosper."

And after that no one thought anything but ill of her and her family.

Ill begotten gain brings sorrow, not happiness.

While these Norse pioneers had some bad characters among them, as illustrated above, they also had many people of good will and good deeds. This was illustrated by what happened to Thorstein, Eric's third son and Freydis' brother, after their unsuccessful attempt to reach Vinland. They had battled bad weather and contrary winds, and as the Saga relates it:

Eventually, a week before winter, they made land at the Western Settlement. Thorstein (who was from the Eastern Settlement) looked for accommodations and found lodgings for all his crew but he and his wife could find none, so the two of them stayed on board the ship for a few days.

They were approached by a man called Thorstein the Black.

"I have come here to invite you and your wife to come and stay with me." Thorstein Erickson replied that he wanted to consult his wife; but Gudrid left the decision to him and he accepted the invitation.

"Then I shall be back tomorrow with a cart to fetch you," said Thorstein the Black. "There is no lack of means to provide for you but you will find life at my house very dull, for there are only the two of us there, my wife and myself, and I am very unsociable. I am also a different faith from yours, although I consider yours to be better than mine."

Leif had converted his family to Christianity; Thorstein the Black remained a pagan worshiping Thor and other ancient gods.

Thorstein, Eric's son, died from an epidemic disease that winter. But Thorstein the Black continued to take care of Gudrid, and in the spring he engaged a crew and sailed her back to her home at Ericksfjord.

The fact that an entire crew of 35 men could be housed in a colony which consisted of only 90 homes at its peak population, and taken care of for the entire winter, speaks for the hospitality of the community as a whole.

The next incident to be related had to do with Karlsefni's dealings with the Skraelings. The latter had initiated an exchange program, trading furs for milk. Later they were back again, in greater numbers, and one of them tried to steal a Norseman's weapons. He was promptly killed.

The Skraelings fled as fast as they could leaving their clothing and furs behind.

"Now we must devise a plan," said Karlsefni, "for I expect they will pay us a third visit, and this time with hostility and in greater numbers."

Karlsefni knew human nature for this is indeed exactly what did happen and a pitched battle ensued. The Norse won, but also lost some of their people, resulting in the decision to return to Greenland.

Throughout history violence has brought on retribution.

But acts of kindness also bring on a like response of goodwill. One of the great lessons taught me in our times was by a colored gentleman (who would now be described as black) meeting in an auditorium in Atlanta during the Civil Rights upheavel when he said, "I have lived and I have worked in the North; I have lived and I have worked in the South; I have always treated other people with respect; and they have always treated me with respect."

People respond in kind.

In another encounter Karlsefni and his crew had come across a small group of natives while they were sleeping. He immediately killed all five, reckoning that "these five must be outlaws and killed them." As discussed earlier, it appears that some of the outlaws from Scandinavia and Iceland had found their way to the American coast by this time. In the Norse system of "outlawing" the desirable feature is not keeping people incarcerated within institutions where they become embittered and more knowledgable about committing other crimes, but it also presents the problem of exposing the law-abiding citizens to the criminal; likewise, the outlaw is exposed to the acts of the citizens who may inflict any sort of harm upon him. Thus we have a "fear of the unknown" type problem with the citizen thinking "kill or be killed." It may have been an overreaction, but then again it may not have been. An equitable and constructive penal system is something we have yet to design.

Eric himself had fled Iceland as an outlaw for having killed a man in a dispute over personal property which he had lost. Prior to that his father had been outlawed from Norway. In recounting the circumstances of Eric's trial (re-membering that the Sagas are not impartial), it would seem that he did not get a fair decision. This is another area where we still have work to do in perfecting an equitable system of justice.

VIII

Significance

What, if anything, Columbus learned from the Norse has been largely discredited, blaming his account of a visit to Iceland. This is recorded in his son's biography, written as he states from his dad's notes. Here is the English translation of that statement verbatim:

In the month of February, 1477, I sailed one hundred leagues beyond the island of Tile, its northern part is in latitude 73° north, and not 63° as some affirm; nor does it lie upon the meridian where Ptolemy says the West begins, but much further west. And to this island, which is as big as England, the English come with their wares especially from Bristol. When I was there, the sea was not frozen, but the tides were so great that in some places they rose 26 fathoms, and fell as much in depth.[70]

Tile is one of the spellings of Thule. In Latin, it is often stated as Ultima Thule or "ultimate land."

The problem with the statement is that Iceland does not lie at 73° N. but instead it is between the 63rd and 67th parallels.

The second puzzling factor is the statement as regards tides inasmuch as the tides in Iceland do not rise to these heights.

The first tendency as regards latitude is to think of Jan Mayen Island, which is north of Iceland. However, that island is at 71°, and not 73°.

Columbus proved his worth as a navigator on his voyage to America and return. Having crossed the ocean, and then sailed half way back, he had covered some 7,000 miles of open water; heading his ship for the tiny island of Santa Maria, the southernmost of the Azores, and a target only four miles wide, he came directly to it. Furthermore he did so within one day's sail of his estimated arrival time, which is most remarkable in days when there was no mechanical way of measuring longitude while at sea. It all depended upon dead-reckoning navigation.

Therefore it is hard to understand how Columbus could have made a mistake of 10 degrees in latitude which corresponds to 600 nautical miles. Did son Ferdinand transcribe the notes correctly?

At this time in history Iceland had been settled by the Norse people and the name they gave it was in common usage among the cartographers of the day. By coincidence, in the Norse languages it is spelled with an "S" instead of a "C." That is, the Icelandic name of their country is spelled "Island," exactly the same spelling as the English word for island. Likewise the Spanish used the letter "s" in their "Isla." Now, if the original notes were not punctuated (or Ferdinand was doing a condensation and assumed that "island" and "Tile" meant the same thing), then it is possible that the reading should be "I sailed 100 leagues beyond Iceland. Tile, whose northern part is in latitude 73° north, etc." Tile would then be used as a descriptive term, in its original meaning.

Now let's have a look at the map. Northward it is possible to sail 100 leagues beyond Iceland, even in February. Furthermore, at 73° and almost due north from Reykjavik is a body of land, an eastern tip of Greenland. Now note that Columbus is giving two specifics: 100 leagues is the distance, and 73° north is the location above Iceland. The size of a league varied with different navigators in earlier times, but Columbus made clear in his *Journal* that he used four nautical miles per league. Chart 27 illustrates the accuracy of Columbus' statement.

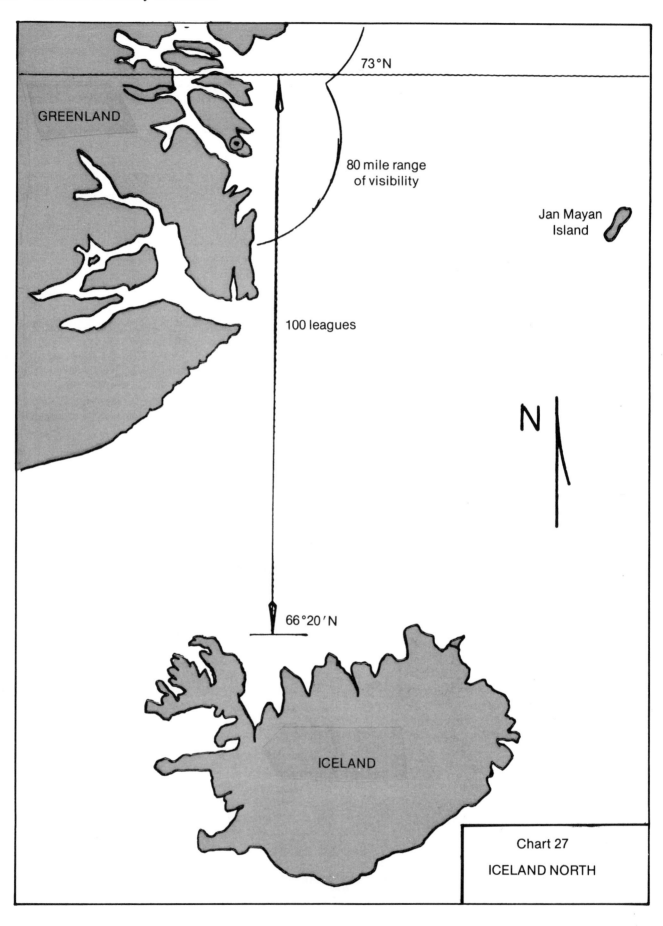

73°N

GREENLAND

80 mile range
of visibility

Jan Mayan
Island

100 leagues

N

66°20′N

ICELAND

Chart 27

ICELAND NORTH

It would not have been possible to have reached this coast in February because the sea is frozen out from Greenland some 50 miles minimum. Even though land cannot be reached (that is except over the ice), it can be seen: The coastal mountains reach elevations of over 5,000 feet and this height on the Earth's curvature table (Appendix B) can be seen for 80 nautical miles out to sea.

This next brings us to Columbus' statement, "Nor does it lie upon the Meridian where Ptolemy says the West begins, but much further west." Ptolemy was a Greek geographer of the second century A.D. whose method of projecting spherical data onto a flat surface (called by cartographers "projections") was still in use through Europe during the time of Columbus. Ptolemy, on his map, had shown Iceland (which he labeled Thule) 15 degrees east of the Bristol, England meridian. Actually the centerline of Iceland is some 10 degrees west of the Bristol meridian, a total difference of 25°—as Columbus said "much further west."

The statement "And to this island, which is as big as England, the English come with their wares, especially from Bristol" is accurate both geographically and historically, as is known from sources in Bristol itself.

The last statement "When I was there, the sea was not frozen, but the tides were so great that in some places they rose 26 fathoms, and fell as much in depth." This is obviously a mixup between fathoms and feet as no place on earth has tides of 26 fathoms. Even so, it does not fit Iceland, and as previously pointed out this would have been incorrect. But the statement, in the sequence of these quoted notes, follows his reference to Bristol. And here at Bristol they do have tides on the Avon River estuary which sometimes rise as much as 40 feet above mean sea level.

Rather than discrediting Columbus and deprecating the value of his knowledge of the north, it should be recognized that this navigational data is accurate to a high degree of precision and proves out Columbus' working knowledge of the northern area.

Other objections to giving the Norse any credit for information obtained there in Iceland are the questions of could the Saga information be translated and whether he docked in Iceland. In the sailing ship days, the need for fresh water alone was sufficient reason to have stopped at Iceland. Logically, the purpose of the voyage to begin with was to go to Iceland. As to the question raised of "translating," it must be noted that both priests and cartographers were trained in and used Latin as a matter of everyday practice. There was simply no problem here.

As to Vinland not being named, it is clear throughout Columbus' enterprise that he was seeking lands to the south and not the lands up in the northwest sector of the ocean; the latter would only have been an indication of the location of the former.

Back to Ferdinand, Columbus' son states in the chapter titled "The Second Reason that Encouraged the Admiral to Seek to Discover the Indies" that many learned men said that one could sail westward from the western end of Africa and Spain to the eastern end of India." One who he quoted was Seneca who wrote "There will come a time in the later years when ocean shall loosen the bounds by which we have been confined, when an immense land shall be revealed and Tiphys shall disclose new worlds, and Thule will no longer be the most remote of countries." Notice that here the name Thule is directly associated with "the most remote of countries," the same manner in which I believe Columbus used it.

In the same chapter, Ferdinand includes his father's reference to a geography book of Julius Capitolinus, quoting "According to the philosophers and Pliny, the ocean which lies between Spain and Africa on the west and India on the east, is not of very great extent and doubtless could be navigated in a few days in a fair wind. Therefore the beginnings of India and the East cannot be very far from the end of Africa and the west." Notice how this ties directly to the quotation in the Iceland geography book which states "To the south of Greenland lies Helluland, then Markland; and from there it is not far to Vinland, which some people think extends from Africa." The manuscript on this dates from approximately 1300 A.D. and so the book, and the information within it, was available in Iceland at the time of Columbus' visit.

Columbus' trip to Iceland, and whatever information he obtained there, does not take away from the credit due him for his accomplishment. He was an intelligent and inquisitive man, compiling information to support his theory that Asia could be reached by sailing west. The information of the Norse, then available in Iceland, that land beyond Vinland continued south for a long distance, maybe as far as Africa, was exactly the kind of information he would have been seeking.

Both he and other cartographers of his time thought that the lands at the northwest corner of the Atlantic Ocean were the northeastern coast of Asia. This is illustrated on Martin Behaim's globe, constructed in 1492, the same year Columbus sailed from Spain (but before his return in 1493).

As it happens both continents taper in a southwesterly direction down to tropical peninsulas at their southeastern corners. Below and to the east of each are a number of islands: the West Indies and the East Indies, respectively.

Richard W. Stephenson, head of the Reference and Bibliography section of the Library of Congress, which includes the geography and map division, has said, "The Behaim globe illustrates for us the concept of the world held by Europeans at the time of Columbus."[71]

Whether or not he had visited Iceland itself cannot be ascertained by present records, but in any event, it shows the importance he attached to Iceland which was the storehouse of information on western seas and lands. The Norse

Sagas continue to be located in Iceland and today are kept there in special quarters.

The Europeans had known of the Asian area through the travels of Marco Polo, at the time of Columbus. So the mixup is understandable. The mapmakers in general, and not just Columbus, thought that these lands to the west were Asia.

Columbus may have actually made that voyage to Iceland or he may have done it vicariously as a cartographer and learned of their knowledge through others. The Norse discoveries in the north were simply a confirmation of the concept of Asia extending to the western shores of the North Atlantic.

Columbus did discover America, both in the sense of the Spanish colonization which followed, and in an overall sense inasmuch as the success of the Spanish encouraged the efforts of others.

Between the time of the Norse discovery and the Spanish discovery Europeans developed (or copied from the Chinese) two inventions which were to change the course of history:

1. Gunpowder. Now the European would dominate the Amerindian as their two cultures overlapped;
2. The Printing Press. Columbus publicized his claim by letters which were printed on Gutenberg's new presses (invented in 1450 A.D.). Now, all of Europe would know, and continue to know, about the lands to the west.

To the Portuguese

The Portuguese in their age of exploration deemed the Norse findings to be of significance for when he looked westward beyond the Azores, King Alfonso of Portugal invoked his friendship with King Christian I of Denmark and Norway to promote a joint voyage of exploration. A combined effort ensued circa 1472–73 in which a trusted nobleman Joao Vaz Corte Real, represented Portugal; Didrik Pining and a man by the name of Pothorst, both of whom were Germans in Danish service, served as captains along with the Scandinavian pilot named Scolvus (some believe him to have been Polish). Pining was later named Governor of Iceland and Corte Real returned to the Azores where he was named Governor of Terceira in 1474. The land they "discovered" would subsequently be called "the land of Corte Real" by the Portuguese.

Not only did they go there originally in conjunction with the Norse (Danish) people, but it remained for a Scandinavian, Sophus Larsen, the Royal Librarian at Copenhagen, to gather the facts of the joint venture and publish same.[72]

Labrador is named for another Portuguese explorer, also from the Azores, and his nickname continues. On the other hand the "Land of Corte Real" was discontinued as the English under Henry VII sent forth John Cabot and claimed it as "New Found Land." Their maritime powers thereafter enabled them to conquer the entire island (the French had been in possession of large parts of it in the interim), as well as make the name stick.

To the Portuguese, Corte Real was the discoverer of America, and the year of discovery was 1472. They continue to send fishing ships to the Grand Banks off Newfoundland and the cod fish caught there is a staple of their diet.

Joao Fernandes (Labrador) sailed far to the north before turning west on his voyage of discovery instead of simply heading northwest which would have been the shorter route, thus indicating acquired knowledge of the North Atlantic. The direct route bucks headwinds; the route north has the advantage of sidewinds, then as they turn west, more variable winds at a higher latitude for shorter crossing.

Since the Scandinavian people had led them here, the earlier discoveries of the Norse do have some significance to the Portuguese.

Christopher Columbus worked in Portugal during this period of exploration, as a cartographer (map maker).

To the French

Jacques Cartier explored the Gulf of St. Lawrence on behalf of the King of France in the year 1534. It was from this mission that the French colonization of Canada subsequently evolved. This navigator arrived about midway on the east coast of Newfoundland and then proceeded northward to the northern entrance of the Strait of Belle Isle. Here he had to wait for the ice to open up before he could enter. Cartier was unaware of the wider, and open, southern entrance to the Gulf had he turned south.

In no way can this approach to North America be construed as "following Columbus." Columbus was never in the area. Instead the Scandinavian knowledge continued as is seen in the map drawn by Stephansson. Cartier headed for what must have been for him a known entryway and waited for it to open. This knowledge was known to the Norse. It was also known to the Portuguese, but it must be remembered that they gained this information through the joint venture with Danes and thereby took advantage of their knowledge of the area. One other possibility is that the French gained it through the English inasmuch as John Cabot's return from his voyage in 1497 was well publicized at the King's Court in London to many foreign emissaries.

It is likely that the French knew about it from both sources. But the fact that he headed for the northern promontory gives credance to the Norse evidence prevailing, inasmuch as this was their approach and in fact this is the only part of Newfoundland to show on Stephansson's map.

To Heredity

The third area of the significance of the Norse voyages is in the people who are descended from them. To whatever extent the Norse infiltrated the Amerindian tribes of North America, they do appear to have had some influence here. The Iroquois, built long houses in the fashion of the Norse, had a legal system similar to the Norse, and enjoyed an advanced system of agriculture. The Iroquois lived on both sides of the St. Lawrence.

In our Northeastern states lived the Algonquin tribes, many of whose people were described by the colonists of the 17th century as "white" and whose languages contained Norse words according to at least some of the students on the subject.

While integrated into larger native populations, their genes continued to produce "white Indians" as the colonists of the 1600's described them. In turn we have known that a number of those became integrated into our present day "white" American. Will Rogers is probably the most famous case: although a Cherokee Indian, his appearance was no different than that of other hundreds of thousands of Europeans who followed his ancestors to these shores. In Georgia it has now become socially acceptable to admit one's parentage includes Indian blood. And yet many of these Indian bloodlines continue to look like other Europeans.

For All of Us

Fourth, and not least of these points in significance, is the lessons that the Sagas can teach us in human relationships. We are still undergoing a process of various races trying to learn to live together. As has been said, if we do not learn the lessons of history we are condemned to repeat them.

APPENDIX A

Medieval Sailing Ship Speeds (Distances)

Early people using the seas quoted distances in terms of the number of days sailing. It must be understood that this referred to the number of days with favorable wind, and did not mean the total time enroute. This is illustrated in the Landnamabok's accounting of the first Norse settlement in Iceland wherein it is stated "learned men said 'it is seven days' sail from Stad in Norway to Horn in the East of Iceland,' but in rough weather it could take much longer." For example if a ship had three days of following winds, with two days of calm, followed by four days of unfavorable winds, then four more days of favorable winds; the journey would still be counted as "seven days' sail." Here is a table of recorded speeds and their sources.

Norse/Scandinavian Voyaging from the *Landnamabok*

Snaefellsness, Iceland to Cape Farwell, Greenland

Days	Miles	Winds	Miles per Day
4	555	Variable	139

Raykjaness, Iceland to Slyne Head, Ireland

5	755	Side to Following	151

Langaness, Iceland to Jan Mayen Island

4	330	Uncharted	83

The source *Diciul Liber De Mansura Obis Terrae,* 825 A.D. (Diciul was the Irish monk "scholar in residence" at the Court of Charlemagne.)

Orkney Islands to Faeroe Islands

1.67	169	Side	101

Great Britian to Iceland

6	441	Side to Head	73.5

From the above, average speeds for the different angles of the wind, rounded off:

Head to Side 75 miles per day
Side Wind area 100 miles per day
Side to Following 150 miles per day

Following wind—by interpolation this would be 200 miles per day. However we have no specific example of this, and in the one instance in the Sagas where it was clearly indicated and could have been measured, "Bjarni ordered his men to shorten sail and not go harder than the ship and rigging could stand." For the purpose of this study, therefore, 150 miles per day is calculated as the maximum speed.

APPENDIX B

Tables of Visibility Range

				Distance of the Horizon				
Height feet	Nautical miles	Statute miles	Height feet	Nautical miles	Statute miles	Height feet	Nautical miles	Statute miles
1	1.1	1.3	120	12.5	14.4	940	35.1	40.4
2	1.6	1.9	125	12.8	14.7	960	35.4	40.8
3	2.0	2.3	130	13.0	15.0	980	35.8	41.2
4	2.3	2.6	135	13.3	15.3	1,000	36.2	41.6
5	2.6	2.9	140	13.5	15.6	1,100	37.9	43.7
6	2.8	3.2	145	13.8	15.9	1,200	39.6	45.6
7	3.0	3.5	150	14.0	16.1	1,300	41.2	47.5
8	3.2	3.7	160	14.5	16.7	1,400	42.8	49.3
9	3.4	4.0	170	14.9	17.2	1,500	44.3	51.0
10	3.6	4.2	180	15.3	17.7	1,600	45.8	52.7
11	3.8	4.4	190	15.8	18.2	1,700	47.2	54.3
12	4.0	4.6	200	16.2	18.6	1,800	48.5	55.9
13	4.1	4.7	210	16.6	19.1	1,900	49.9	57.4
14	4.3	4.9	220	17.0	19.5	2,000	51.2	58.9
15	4.4	5.1	230	17.3	20.0	2,100	52.4	60.4
16	4.6	5.3	240	17.7	20.4	2,200	53.7	61.8
17	4.7	5.4	250	18.1	20.8	2,300	54.9	63.2
18	4.9	5.6	260	18.4	21.2	2,400	56.0	64.5
19	5.0	5.7	270	18.8	21.6	2,500	57.2	65.8
20	5.1	5.9	280	19.1	22.0	2,600	58.3	67.2
21	5.2	6.0	290	19.5	22.4	2,700	59.4	68.4
22	5.4	6.2	300	19.8	22.8	2,800	60.5	69.7
23	5.5	6.3	310	20.1	23.2	2,900	61.6	70.9
24	5.6	6.5	320	20.5	23.6	3,000	62.7	72.1
25	5.7	6.6	330	20.8	23.9	3,100	63.7	73.3
26	5.8	6.7	340	21.1	24.3	3,200	64.7	74.5
27	5.9	6.8	350	21.4	24.6	3,300	65.7	75.7
28	6.1	7.0	360	21.7	25.0	3,400	66.7	76.8
29	6.2	7.1	370	22.0	25.3	3,500	67.7	77.9
30	6.3	7.2	380	22.3	25.7	3,600	68.6	79.0
31	6.4	7.3	390	22.6	26.0	3,700	69.6	80.1
32	6.5	7.5	400	22.9	26.3	3,800	70.5	81.2
33	6.6	7.6	410	23.2	26.7	3,900	71.4	82.2
34	6.7	7.7	420	23.4	27.0	4,000	72.4	83.3
35	6.8	7.8	430	23.7	27.3	4,100	73.3	84.3
36	6.9	7.9	440	24.0	27.6	4,200	74.1	85.4
37	7.0	8.0	450	24.3	27.9	4,300	75.0	86.4
38	7.1	8.1	460	24.5	28.2	4,400	75.9	87.4
39	7.1	8.2	470	24.8	28.6	4,500	76.7	88.3
40	7.2	8.3	480	25.1	28.9	4,600	77.6	89.3
41	7.3	8.4	490	25.3	29.2	4,700	78.4	90.3
42	7.4	8.5	500	25.6	29.4	4,800	79.3	91.2
43	7.5	8.6	520	26.1	30.0	4,900	80.1	92.2
44	7.6	8.7	540	26.6	30.6	5,000	80.9	93.1
45	7.7	8.8	560	27.1	31.2	6,000	88.6	102.0
46	7.8	8.9	580	27.6	31.7	7,000	95.7	110.2
47	7.8	9.0	600	28.0	32.3	8,000	102.3	117.8
48	7.9	9.1	620	28.5	32.8	9,000	108.5	124.9
49	8.0	9.2	640	28.9	33.3	10,000	114.4	131.7
50	8.1	9.3	660	29.4	33.8	15,000	140.1	161.3
55	8.5	9.8	680	29.8	34.3	20,000	161.8	186.3
60	8.9	10.2	700	30.3	34.8	25,000	180.9	208.2
65	9.2	10.6	720	30.7	35.3	30,000	198.1	228.1
70	9.6	11.0	740	31.1	35.8	35,000	214.0	246.4
75	9.9	11.4	760	31.5	36.3	40,000	228.8	263.4
80	10.2	11.8	780	31.9	36.8	45,000	242.7	279.4
85	10.5	12.1	800	32.4	37.3	50,000	255.8	294.5
90	10.9	12.5	820	32.8	37.7	60,000	280.2	322.6
95	11.2	12.8	840	33.2	38.2	70,000	302.7	348.4
100	11.4	13.2	860	33.5	38.6	80,000	323.6	372.5
105	11.7	13.5	880	33.9	39.1	90,000	343.2	395.1
110	12.0	13.8	900	34.3	39.5	100,000	361.8	416.5
115	12.3	14.1	920	34.7	39.9	200,000	511.6	589.0

APPENDIX C

Assessments of Paul H. Chapman's
The Man Who Led Columbus to America

Library Journal:

Presenting a convincing and logical hypothesis, Chapman claims that Columbus planned his trans-Atlantic route from the voyages of St. Brendan of Ireland (about 565 A.D.) which are described in the medieval manuscript *Navigatio Sancti Brendani Abbatis,* but are usually regarded as mythical. Instead of taking the shortest route from the "Gates of Hercules," Columbus first headed south to the Canaries where he changed the Nina's riggings so the ship could sail with the trade winds. Using this route, Columbus crossed in 36 days (the Mayflower took 64 for the shorter direct route). Chapman believes Columbus knew how to find the trade winds from St. Brendan's trips. The author uses his knowledge of navigation and cartography plus the descriptions in the *Navigatio* to chart St. Brendan's reputed voyages and figure out his destinations. Photographs of the areas, simplified charts, maps, and illustrations add persuasive details to this well-researched account. The text which alternates translated quotes from the *Navigatio* in italics with Chapman's comments, will add an interesting dimension to collections on early explorations of the New World.

The Ensign:

Stated simply, the author contends not only that Columbus did *not* discover America, but that he followed the track to America and back of the man who *did*—St. Brendan, The Navigator.

The author first became curious about the Columbus story while majoring in history at Furman University. His navigational training and experience while ferrying planes across the Atlantic (1942–1945) helped him visualize the possibility. Visiting the Faeroes, Iceland, Ireland, and Spain at a later

date confirmed his reading. Chapman is convinced that St. Brendan led the way.

Citing the availability to Columbus of copies of the book describing St. Brendan's voyage, which is estimated to have taken place between January, 564 and August, 565, A.D., Chapman presents a strong case. By plotting each leg of St. Brendan's epic voyage, the reader, particularly one acquainted with navigation, can follow the author's reconstruction—and accept his logic that Columbus, as a cartographer-navigator, would recognize a workable route when he saw one.

Chapman concludes this interesting book with a statement that he is not discrediting Columbus. He is merely attempting to establish the fact that St. Brendan and his 14 fellow monks served as "scouts" in their 40-foot currach-type vessel.

The Man Who Led Columbus to America certainly deserves a place in the History Section of the Ship's Library.

NEARA Journal (New England Antiquities Research Association):

Written by Mr. Chapman before he became a Journal reader, this attractive volume is nevertheless a sterling example of the type of scholarship—thorough and exacting, yet bold and imaginative—that NEARA approves and encourages; and it is with pleasure that we unhesitatingly recommend it to anyone with the slightest interest in pre-Columbian trans-Atlantic crossings.

Mr. Chapman's subject is the voyage by the Irish abbot St. Brendan and his crew of monks, undertaken in a currach or woodframed boat covered with leather hides, approximately 560 A.D.; which voyage penetrated far into the Atlantic basin and almost certainly touched the shores of America. There are more than 120 medieval manuscripts (Latin) versions still extant of the "Navigation of Brendan," testifying to the impact that the voyage had on European thinking for nearly ten centuries. With assistance from learned and competent scholars, Mr. Chapman has collated these varying versions of the "Navigation," and has reconstructed the voyage with a high degree of accuracy and plausibility.

The first serious effort along these lines was made 16 years ago by British author and former NEARA member, Geoffrey Ashe, in his *Land to the West;* while it still stands as a splendid pioneering attempt, and will be a necessary item for all Brendan students to consult, Mr. Chapman's work definitely supersedes it. This reviewer can think of no higher commendation. Briefly, the Chapman thesis is that the Brendan Voyage was from southwest Ireland north to the Faeroes, then doubling back to the Azores, and from there—taking advantage of the Canaries and North Equatorial Currents—to Barbados and Barbuda in the outer West Indies. Following the Antillean Current to the Bahamas, Brendan's currach then drifted into the Gulf Stream and was carried past Newfoundland to Iceland. From there, Brendan returned to Ireland, stopping at the tiny islet of Rockall on the way.

Every step of this route is buttressed by impressive geographic and navigational evidence. It is probably as close as we can ever come to ascertaining Brendan's actual itinerary. Moreover, Mr. Chapman makes out a very convincing case that Columbus, through his studies of the Brendan Navigation manuscripts, was aware of both the North Equatorial Current as a carrier of vessels across the Atlantic from the Canaries to the West Indies, and of the Gulf Stream as the return current for regaining Europe. In other words, Columbus was able to actually plan to a very large extent the actual route of his epic First Voyage, before ever setting sail. The title of Mr. Chapman's excellent book derives from this assertion that Columbus took Brendan as his guide.

Southwest Airlines Magazine:

Author Paul Chapman, an experienced pilot and navigator, used his skills and his knowledge of cartography to decipher the logs, notes and thoughts of Columbus. Chapman had long heard stories from his Irish-American friends how the new world had actually been discovered by their ancestors . . . years ahead of Columbus. Chapman's amusement turned to curiosity when he began digging into ancient texts detailing geographical descriptions of the western Atlantic of which they could have had no knowledge.

Through the centuries, Christopher Columbus' biographers have been amiss to explain how Columbus obtained the route he sailed to the Americas. Columbus did not discover America by sailing west from Spain! Nor did he get home by sailing east . . . and he did not follow his route out on his route back. Though his food and water were limited, he did not sail the shortest possible routes. Why did he choose the long way, and how did he come to know of the complicated route plans?

It is fact that prior to his voyage to the new world, Columbus once sailed to Iceland, where he was privy to the Sagas of ancient Norsemen who sailed to lands west of the then-known world; but these new lands were not the mystic East which Columbus was seeking. It is also recorded that he ventured to Galway Bay in Ireland. Here the story was told that St. Brendan, the navigator, had found land to the west and this looked most promising to Columbus.

Is it possible that Columbus, himself alone with only Divine guidance, could have deduced the secrets of the trade winds and ocean currents essential to the success of his voyage? Paul Chapman thinks not, and supports his theories with a tremendous amount of evidence, both actual and circumstantial. His thesis hinges upon St. Brendan's journey, and the occurrences that go with it . . . the first written reports of an iceberg, a submarine volcano eruption, a coral sea, grapefruit, sea grapes and the island group of the Faeroes, the Azores, the Antilles and the Bahamas.

Others, Briefly

Our Sunday Visitor:

(Chapman) does an admirable job of matching photos to Brendan's descriptions and makes a plausible case for his theory.

Edwin H. Halvorsen, retired sea captain:

I have enjoyed every reading minute of it. I think it is excellent.

Carl Selmer, Hunter College, author of *Navigatio Sancti Brendani Abbatis:*

"I was deeply impressed by your book. You have accomplished something extraordinary, something no one ever has done in spite of all efforts. You have definitely proved that Brendan discovered America, at least the island group, and that Columbus used Brendan's plan for his voyage."

W. A. Newsome, Jr., Chief, Navigation Division, U.S. Air Force Academy:

"I found the material plausible and interesting; your substantiation is well researched and convincing, having been to most of the pertinent locations during my traveling life."

Michael Devenish, Editor, Oxford University Press (England):

"As a sailor and (amateur) navigator myself, I found your manuscript on Columbus and St. Brendan utterly intriguing."

Sailing Magazine:

. . . the ardent Columbians of Genoa will scorn Chapman's argument, but in time even they will have to come to the thought that his stature as discoverer of the New World rests more on his achievement of being the right man at the right time . . . Columbus did leave a mark, far more enduring than the wooden crosses he erected on his Indies, and if St. Brendan helped make this possible, as Chapman thinks, let him be honored as well.

N. L. Hersey, Church Management:

"The book opened up a whole new horizon of history for me. It is a well-documented and researched treatise on the travels of Saint Brendan. His writings and account of his voyage to Barbados and the Bahamas in 564–565 A.D. gave Columbus valuable knowledge of currents and winds which he used to good advantage in his voyage of 1492.

Statistical and geographic data make the book a fascinating bit of history that has been too often forgotten."

James Travis, University of Alabama Press:

. . . *"The Man Who Led Columbus to America* . . . was originally submitted for publication to the University of Alabama Press . . . It was approved for publication by our press committee, having been strongly endorsed by Professor Cyrus Gordon of Brandeis University, the orientalist and a leading authority on pre-Columbian crossings of the Atlantic. Plans for publication fell through, however . . . As managing editor, I regard Alabama's loss of this publication opportunity as most unfortunate, for Chapman's book is academically sound, highly interesting, and should make a strong impression in both Europe and the Americas, with specialists and readers, alike."

Notes

Chapter I—The Problem

1. *National Geographic,* November 1964, Vol. 126, No. 5, pp. 708–734.
2. Sauer, *Northern Mists,* Berkeley, University of California Press, 1968, p. 137.
3. Ceram, *The First American,* Harcourt Brace Jovanovich, New York, 1971, pp. 22–28.
4. Ingstad, *Westward to Vinland,* New York, St. Martin's Press, 1969.
5. Morison, *The European Discovery of America, The Northern Voyages,* Oxford University Press, New York, 1971, p. 38.
6. Magnusson, *Viking Expansion Westwards,* Henry C. Walk, Inc., New York, 1973, p. 143, 147–8.
7. Annals of the Association of American Geographers, December 1979, p. 806.

Chapter II—Tools for Solving the Problem

8. "A Conference on Writing in America Before Columbus" sponsored by Columbus College of the University of Georgia System, October 18–20, 1979.
9. Op. Cit., pp. 716–717.
10. Chapman, *The Man Who Led Columbus to America,* Judson Press (now One Candle Press) Atlanta, Georgia, 1973.
11. Ducuil, *Measurements of the Earth,* The Dublin Institute for Advanced Studies, Dublin, 1967, pp. 75–77.
12. The Norse have been noted for building a "clinker" ship. This simply refers to the method of applying the siding in an overlapping fashion, rather than the butt-to-butt arrangement of these boards, utilized elsewhere in Europe. It did not change the configuration of the ship.
13. Hernar is at 60° 41′ N (19′ south of 61°); the northernmost Shetland Island reaches 60° 50′ N, with a visibility range from its northern peaks of 25 nautical miles, thereby visible up to 61° 15′ N; the southernmost Faeroes Island is at 61° 24′ N, with a visibility from its peak of 44 nautical miles, and therefore the peak is visible down to 60° 40′ N; from 61 degrees N the mariners would see the peak down to the 440 foot level; the peak here is 1,539 feet—elsewhere the land drops down below the 1,000 foot contour, and thus would appear "half sunk below the horizon;" southernmost Iceland is at 63° 23′ N or 143 miles north of the 61st parallel—we had estimated the ships speed at 150 nautical miles per day (Appendix A) and the text of this statement is "a days sail south of Iceland."
14. Did the Norseman of the early 11th century have the use of a sextant for navigation purposes? The Sagas do not say so specifically. But in several instances they show an awareness of latitudinal distances and/or location. This may have been accomplished by "eye balling" the height of the north star—in a similar fashion to that practiced by the Polynesians in the Pacific.

    Bjorn Landstrom, author of *Columbus,* (see Bibliography) pointed out to me during a personal conversation on this subject that human hands on outstretched arms can be used to measure angles of altitudes in the sky, just as horses are still measured as "so many hands" in height.

    But the precision shown by their knowledge of the parallel sailing technique (above) is such that I am led to believe that they did it with instruments similar to the astrolobes (sextants) known to have been in use elsewhere in Europe. Just as ships were of a common design from the Mediterranean in the south to the Baltic in the north, so were ships equipment. Two clues point toward the use of the sextant:
    a. We know they used a ship bearing dial, and one of these has been found at the Greenland colony site. This instrument functions just like the sextant in measuring the relative angle of a heavenly body to the ship, but does it on a horizontal plane, whereas the sextant measures the angle on a vertical plane. Again, the Sagas do not mention this instrument specifically, but refer to the ships "bearings." A picture of the ships bearing dial can be found in the National Geographic article, Op. Cit., p. 712.

    However, finding the ships bearing is not limited to a noontime shadow line as the picture caption in that article would indicate. The ancients well knew the relative position of the sun at other times of the day, as shown in their use of the terms "summer sunset" to indicate northwest and "winter sunset" for southwest, "summer sunrise" for northeast and "winter sunrise" for southeast. An experienced observer could judge by the time of day the sun position and thereby obtain the ship's approximate bearing.
    b. A letter written in the year 1266 by a priest called Halldor describes traveling in Greenland to a latitude of 75° 46′ North. Since this was given in both degrees and minutes, a sextant at that time would have been a necessity, and it had to be an advanced model capable of calibrating this finely. Our instruments during World War II could do no better. (One minute of latitude equals one nautical mile.)

    This leaves remaining the question why no sextants have been found among the artifacts. There are two sources from which most of the Norse sailing ship artifacts have been recovered: one is the channel nearby Roskilde, Denmark and the other is the grave site area in southern Norway.

In the first instance, the ships were emptied of all removable parts—even the masts—and then loaded with stones to form a channel barrier. Thus, no artifacts, except the ships themselves, have been recovered here.

In the second instance, the ships have been found in burial mounds. Here the artifacts have been plentiful as the corpses were supplied with goods for a later life but since the Norse equivalent of heaven was secured, there was no need for instruments to find the way. The Norse, being a practical people, did in my opinion, continue to use these instruments and even those found centuries later would have been thought of as "antiques" rather than "artifacts."

The Greenland latitudinal measurement related above comes from *The Story of Einar Sokkson* and is related in Magnusson's *The Vinland Sagas,* (see Bibliography) p. 21.

Chapter III—Courses

15. Airplanes normally take off and land against the wind to give them more lift going up and more braking effect coming down.
16. Sacred Bay at a time of lower land elevations could also qualify as to the visibility range fitting within the statement "at low tide their ship was left high and dry with the coast almost out of sight." Further there is a small lake running through a river into the bay on its southeast corner. However, it does not fit in the overall sense for the following reasons: (a) On Belle Isle the entire land mass of this northern promontory would have been seen, and the statement as to sailing around the headland would therefore be applicable going into Pistolet Bay on the right hand side of the land mass rather than into Sacred Bay which is within the land mass; (b) Sacred Bay arriving from the north, is dotted with rocks on the north side, several of which rise up out of the water and form small islands, so I doubt that the Norse navigators would have attempted to sail their ship in between these (and the Saga does use the term "sailing" rather than rowing); (c) the Saga further tells us that they did this on a westerly course, and since they had been on a north-south course coming down from Belle Isle, the course into Sacred Bay would have been southerly, whereas the course necessary to turn away from these islands and rocks was in keeping with "they steered a westerly course around the headland."
17. *Research in Norway* (see Bibliography), p. 11.
18. Cartier's report is translated into English in *The Discovery of North America* (see Bibliography), pp. 84–97.
19. Throughout the Vinland Sagas these Mariners used compass directions such as "east" and "west" to indicate a turn or a relative position rather than "left" or "right." This terminology was used here in Thorvald's voyage northward as he was heading up the coast of Labrador, he turned eastward rather than westward; then that coast turns northward. Previously, Thorvald's crew sailed west (or turned left) down the Strait of Belle Isle.

This wording again occurs when Thorvald elects to leave Kjalarness. The Saga terms it "eastward" although it more southeastward—but it does make clear which way they went along a given coastline.
20. Gwyn Jones in *The Norse Atlantic Saga* (see Bibliography) p. 48, reports the eastern settlement reached the size of 180 farms and the western settlement had 90 farms.
21. Magnusson and Palsson (Op. Cit., p. 119) date Leif's departure for Vinland as circa 1001 A.D. based on other Icelandic sources giving the date of his father's (Eric the Red) immigration to Greenland as the starting point.

Chapter IV—Clarifications

22. Haklyut's *Divers Voyages,* p. 167.

Chapter VI—Whatever Happened to Them?

23. Magnusson, *The Vinland Sagas,* Op. Cit., p. 18.
24. Ibid, pp. 24–25.

25. Mowat (see Bibliography), p. 34, an English translation quoting the Icelandic *Landnamabok.*
26. Ibid, pp. 296–9, quoting from the *Eyrbyggja Saga.*
27. Ibid, pp. 296–297.
28. English translation, Magnusson's *The Vinland Sagas,* Op. Cit., pp. 26–27.
29. The *Flatey Book,* published by the Norroena Society, London, Stockholm, Copenhagen, Berlin and New York, 1906, and stating "all reproductions are by Royal Danish sanction and the Papal Secretary of State." Fragments referring to American discoveries, pp. 113, 115.
30. Letter from Msgr. Martino Guisti, prefect, Vatican, November 9, 1966 to W. R. Anderson, publisher of *Viking Ship.*
31. The *Flatey Book,* Op. Cit.
32. The *Flatey Book,* Op. Cit., p. 176.
33. Pope Alexander VI appears unaware of the report received in 1448 by a predecessor Pope Nichols V.

These and other references to the Sea of Gardar, from the manuscripts of the Vatican Archives, can be found in *Documents Alecta,* J. C. Haywood, 1893, Rome, translated into English by the Catholic Historical Review, Vol. 3, pp. 210–227.
34. Thor Heyerdahl published this information in both the *Epilogue to* Enterline's *Viking America* (see Bibliography) and in his own book *Early Man and the Ocean,* pp. 178–179 and 138 respectively. In the former he cites Archbishop Eric Valdendorf and the historian Absalon Pedersson Beyer of Bergen as recording these lists independently.
35. Ingstad, *National Geographic,* Op Cit., p. 734: From a study of old documents in the mid-fourteenth century, the learned Icelandic Bishop Gisle Oddsson wrote in 1637 that the Norse inhabitants of Greenland had 'turned to the people of America' (ad Americae populous se converterunt).
36. Beamish, North Ludlow, *The Discovery of America by the Northmen,* London, T. N. W. Boone, 1841, p. 113, refers to a fragment of Bellum Codex, No. 192, p. 290.
37. Ibid, pp. 114–115 quoting the source as Codex, No. 115, p. 293.
38. As stated in Chapter II, the construction of the Portolan Chart has been lost to our knowledge, however several features of it are believed to be understood. I have been working on deciphering it, off and on since 1974, and have succeeded in charting a course across the Atlantic utilizing the example Portolan shown herein as Chart 3. I regret to report however that this does not work on all of the maps. Apparently there is a key which I have not yet found, which changes the plotting with the latitude.
39. *The Discovery of North America,* Op. Cit., p. 83.
40. Catalog 36, 1980, p. 39.
41. NEARA (New England Antiquities Research Association) special publication titled *The Newport Tower: The English Elizabethan Solution,* by Horace F. Silliman published in November, 1979, states on page 2, "a document written in 1632, and usually identified as the Plowden Paper, is a petition for the right to found a colony on Long Island and the adjacent mainland. Among the many resources mentioned as available for exploration in this new land is a 'rownd stone towre' which, as Sir Edmund Plowden, the petitioner, goes on to say, could be occupied by 'idle men as soldiers and gent,' who could 'trucke and trafficke by torne with the savages.' The text makes it clear that the outpost is already in existence and that it is across some water from the main settlement to be planted on Long Island. Since no other tower is known to have existed in New Jersey, Connecticut, or Rhode Island, the inference is that Sir Edmund was refering to the Newport Tower."
42. Ibid, p. 2. Frederick G. Pohl and Hjalmar Holand.
43. *Journal of the Surveying and Mapping Division* of the American Society of Engineers, February, 1960.
44. *The Newport Tower,* Op. Cit., In a supplement on page 27 quotes an account of the tower by Benson J. Lossing, noted historian of the American Revolution, in his *Pictorial Field Book of the Revolution,* Harper and Bros., New York, 1859.
45. The building is 23 feet in diameter, with walls 3 feet thick using 20 feet from center of fireplace to center of windows, and a 3 foot width each for the window and the fire itself, would make a light beam spreading out at a seven degree angle on either side of a center line. This has been utilized in chart 21 showing the angle of the beam.

The tower sits on a hill with its base 85 feet above sea level. An additional 15 feet to the fireplace and window levels makes a 100 foot total elevation. From this height the light is visible down to sea level for a distance of 11.4 miles.

The chart herein shows how the light would serve the mariner. First it identifies the channel to use, and this is important inasmuch as there are four different channels in the immediate area of Narragansett Bay and still others close by; then it helps him to steer within the channel as the beam comes directly down it the land masses protruding on both sides thus become silhouetted.

A light in the south facing window would also serve as a mark for ships approaching from the ocean.

Traces of stucco have been found both inside and outside of the building. A stuccoed building, in the European style, is that which is shown in the picture on the Mercator Map.

46. In Genoa the name was spelled Colombo, in Portugal it was Colom, and Spain, Colon.

47. Buchanan, Donal B., "The Spirit Pond Stones—Hoax or History?" An article published in *Popular Archaeology*, Vol. 4, Nos. 5–6, May–June, 1975, pp. 23 29.

48. HOOB/HOOP usually spelled Hop, but Magnusson uses Hope, indicating a pronunciation with a long "O" and the intent appears in this inscription through the use of the double "O." Phoentic spelling in the Middle Ages was common practice.

It will be noted that, within the Saga, Leif entered a tidal lake but he did not use the word "hope" to describe it. Only Karlsefni uses this word.

Karlsefni's home was on the Skaagafjord in northern Iceland. Some 20 miles to the west, on the next opening to the sea there is a basin which is still called "Hope." Both the National Geographic map on Scandinavia of 1963 and the U.S. Air Force Jet Navigation Chart of 1955 show this to be partially open, partially blocked, similar to present day Hare Bay, Newfoundland. On the Geographic map the one in Iceland is labeled "Ho'p."

49. TEN TWO. Old Norse, like Old English, sometimes used the words for each digit, instead of the combination word. For examples, in English, "four and twenty black birds," in Norse, the Vinland Sagas give the size of Leif's crew literally as "three tens and a half," but it is usually translated "thirty-five."

50. LAG. This word, like many English words, has more than one meaning. We have used the nautical meaning in this instance because it is within that context. Literally, the right or correct position (to the ship)/the rudder in its place.

51. There is another explanation of this plotting which is so simple that it can be done mentally without need of pen and paper. It involves one of the simplest formulas in math: In a 60/30 triangle the side opposite the 60 degree angle is twice as long as the side opposite the 30 degree angle. We know that the ancients used the 5–4–3 triangle to square corners of buildings, which is still used by many homebuilders who understand its use but never heard of the Pythagorean Theorem on which it is based.

Here are the mental steps for the 60/30 triangle which is involved:

a. Southwest Iceland, for which the navigator would aim in sailing from America, lies on the 64 degree north parallel; so does the western settlement of the Norse in Greenland—from which Karlsefni and his colonists took their departure. (Present-day Godthab); so does the Hall peninsula on Baffin Island, which is the next indicated location of the Karlsefni voyage by the analysis within the courses section of this book. Thus, one side of the triangle is the 64th parallel.

b. Karlsefni next moved down the coast of Labrador and his ships bearing instrument would have told him this was at a 60 degree angle to the parallel (although shown in compass points). The distance on this leg amounted to eight days sailing for Karlsefni, but he did some exploration along the way. Utilizing both Bjarni's and Leif's times for Newfoundland/Vinland to South Labrador/Markland, of two days, plus each had said two days for Markland to Helluland/North Labrador, then adding his own two days down from Bjarn Island/Hope Peninsula area would net total six days and this would be the base leg of the triangle.

c. The third leg calls for a 90 degree angle off the base leg which would be a bearing of 60 degrees to true north, and the distance would be twice that of the base leg or twelve days.

Let it be remembered that Karlsefni was famous as a sea trader before making his colonization attempt. His livelihood required expertise in long, open ocean navigation from his home in Iceland. A degree of proficiency was necessary simply to have survived.

In such trading endeavors Karlsefni would have been exposed to the knowledge of others: the sextants and/or astrolobes which were being used elsewhere in Europe; words and letters of the alphabet being used by other peoples.

52. MILTIAKI/MILDAKI. Here is one of the many Norse words with identical English usage for the first syllable; Mild or "gentle"; AKI means field, thus "gentle land."

Translations of these runic words are by Donal B. Buchanan. Source used: *Icelandic-English Dictionary,* Cleasby and Vigfusson, second edition, 1969.

53. *National Geographic,* Op. Cit., p. 734.

54. *Man In the Northeast,* No. 6, Fall 1973, Center Harbor, NH, P. 9.

55. There are many runic writings in America which I feel should be reexamined in the light of these findings as regards to the Spirit Pond Stones. One in particular is the Kensington Stone which was found in western Minnesota. As Donal Buchanan points out in his article (Op. Cit., p. 25) two unusual runic characters appear on both the Spirit Pond Stones and on the Kensington Stone. Since the Kensington Stone has been held in disrepute for the better part of a century by the academic community, surely the would-be faker of the Spirit Pond Stones would not have used the same two letters of the alphabet which had caused the Kensington Stone to be questioned. Conversely, it would appear that with the Spirit Pond Mapstone being validated, this may mean that the Kensington Stone was a valid writing also.

In addition to the lettering on the Kensington Stone, one word concerns the linguists. Samuel Eliot Morison in the *European Discovery of America,* (Op. Cit., p. 76,) calls the Kensington Stone a hoax and says "If you dig up a 'Greek Vase' resting on a telephone book, it is a waste of time to try to prove that the vase is genuine. The Kensington story is preposterous . . . one word alone, opdagelsefard, 'voyage of discovery,' which did not occur in any Scandinavian language for several centuries after 1362, gives it away."

I respectfully submit that neither Morison nor anyone else can possibly know the exact date when this word appeared in any of the Scandinavian languages. The proof of this has been previously shown in the linguists' lack of knowledge of the Old Norse use of the word "woman" in a nautical sense.

Accompanying these notes is a picture of the Kensington Stone and a translation follows.

"Eight Goths and twenty-two Norwegians on an expedition from Vinland Westward. Our camp was by two small islands one days journey north of the stone. We went fishing one day When we came home we found ten men red with blood and dead. AVAM (Ave Maria) deliver us from evil. Have ten men by the sea to look after our ships fourteen days journey from this island. 1362."

A question has been raised as to the expedition containing Goths and Norwegians, traditional enemies. This has been resolved however by H. R. Holand, who found that in the year 1354 King Magnus Erikson of Norway and Sweden had sent out just such an expedition containing both Goths and Norwegians. While little further is known of the expedition, the time element makes it possible that this was one and the same with those who carved the Kensington Stone; and in any event, it disproves the theory that the stone could not have been carved by a mixed expedition.

To those who have argued "this is too far away" from the east coast of America for the Norse to have journeyed, as a navigator I would point out that a ship coming down from the Western Settlement on Greenland via Baffin Island could just as well turn west and go down the Hudson Bay coastline as Karlsefni and his expedition had sailed down the east coast of the same land mass. Flowing into the Hudson Bay is the Red River of the North which comes out of western Minnesota, the location of the Kensington Stone.

As it happens, the first English colony in Manitoba, western Canada, was located in this same Red River Valley. Nearby at Brandon is the site of Ft. Brandon, an early Hudson's Bay Company post.

The sea to which the inscription refers may have been Lake Winnipeg, which is down stream on the Red River, and the fourteen days journey would be appropriate for the distance. Utilizing the same 37½ miles

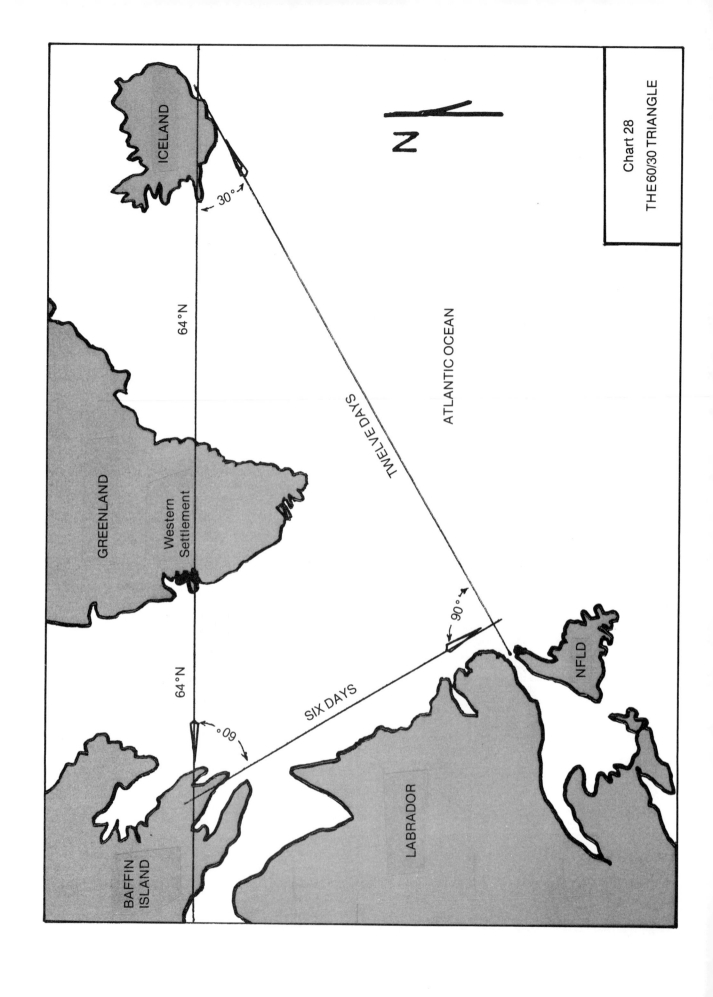

ICELAND

30°

64°N

GREENLAND

Western
Settlement

TWELVE DAYS

ATLANTIC OCEAN

90°

NFLD

64°N

SIX DAYS

60°

BAFFIN
ISLAND

LABRADOR

N

Chart 28
THE 60/30 TRIANGLE

Kensington Stone. The validity of this stone with its Norse runic writing has been argued since its discovery in 1898—frequently with strong statements, pro and con. The author recommends that it now be reexamined in the light of the findings herein on the Maine Spirit Pond Mapstone.

Photo courtesy Alexander, Minnesota Chamber of Commerce.

per day calculated for the voyage of Thorvald's crew in their western coastal exploration, a twelve day journey would cover 525 miles. The distance between Kensington, Minnesota, and Lake Winnipeg "as the crow flies" is 325 miles, which should put it close to the same total distance on the river's route.

* * *

As this book is going to press, I've just learned through the publication *Vikingship* that Dr. Robert A. Hall, Jr., Professor Emeritus of Linguistics, Cornell University, has completed a study to be published shortly entitled "The Kensington Rune-Stone Is Genuine." His letter to W. R. Anderson, editor of the *Vikingship*, concludes, "To my way of thinking the 98% liklihood of the Kensington Stone being genuine is evident in the linguistic material of the text itself."

* * *

56. *Discovery*, McGraw Hill, New York, 1964, pp. 128, 129, 134, 138–142.
57. *The Rediscovery of Lost America*, New York, E. P. Dutton, 1951 and 1979, pp. 53–54.
58. Ibid. pp. 239–242.
59. Ibid. p. 168.
60. Ibid. p. 170.
61. Ibid. pp. 170–188.
62. *The Discovery of North America*, Op. Cit., p. 83.
63. Enterline, Op. Cit., P. 152.
64. Funk and Wagnalls, New York, 1940, 1942.
65. *The Discovery of North America*, Op. Cit., p. 89.
66. Struever and Holton, *Koster*, New York, Doubleday, Signet, 1973 and 1979, p. 10.
67. Chapman, Op. Cit., p. 44. An English translation of the manuscript parts of *Navigatio Sanciti Brendani Abbatis*, Carl Selmer, University of Notre Dame Press, 1959.
68. Letter from Thomas L. Gaffney, Director, Maine Historical Society, to author, states in part "from what little information is available in this library it appears that Maine Indians made their canoes primarily from birch bark, but that hides particularly those of moose, were sometimes used."
69. Don Locke, *Beothuck Artifacts*, privately published and available at the reconstructed Beothuck village.

Chapter VIII—Significance

70. Colon, Ferdinand, *The Life of the Admiral Christopher Columbus*, translated by Benjamin Keen, New Brunswick, New Jersey, Rutgers University Press, 1959, pp. 11, 18, 19.
71. Personal conversation with the author during research on *The Man Who Led Columbus to America*.
72. Sauer, Op. Cit., p. 25. Larsen's book was titled *Discovery of North America Twenty Years Before Columbus*, and published in 1924.

Bibliography

No attempt is being made here to cover all of the writings on these subjects, as it would be massive. Only those referenced herein, and those which the author feels present the broadly held concepts are included. For a more complete list of books on the subject of Vinland the author recommends the article by McManis, cited below.

re Norse Voyaging

Enterline, James Robert, *Viking America*. New York: Doubleday, 1972.

Ingstad, Helge, *Westward to Vinland*, New York, St. Martin's Press, 1969.

Jones, Gwyn, *The Norse Atlantic Saga*. London: Oxford University Press, 1964.

Magnusson, Magnus and Herman Palsson, *The Vinland Sagas*. New York: New York University Press; 1965; (paperback) Penguin Books Ltd.

Magnusson, Magnus, *Viking Expansion Westwards*. New York: Walk, 1973.

Mowart, Farley, *Westviking*. Boston: Little Brown and Company, 1965; in Canada: McClelland and Stewart.

Oxenstierna, Count Eric, *The Norsemen*. Greenwich, CT: New York Graphic Society, 1965.

Pohl, Frederick J, *The Viking Settlements of North America*. New York: Potter, 1972.

(Articles)

Anderson, W. R., Editor of *Vikingship*, Box 301, Chicago, IL 60690, has for 16 years published articles and reports on evidence of Norse presence in America before the time of Columbus.

Ingstad, Helge, "Vinland Ruins Prove Vikings Found the New World," *National Geographic*, Vol. 126, No. 5, November 1964, pp. 708–734.

Lee, Thomas E., "Norse in Ungava," *Anthropological Journal of Canada*, Vol. 17, No. 2, pp 2–48.

McManis, Douglas R., "The Traditions of Vinland," *Annals of the Association of American Geographers*, Vol. 55, No. 4, December 1969, pp. 797–814.

Magnusson, Magnus, "The Ultimate Outpost," *Scandinavian Review*, Vol. 68, No. 1, March 1980, pp. 6–29.

Marstrander, Svene, "Archeological Finds Confirm the Saga Accounts of Vinland," *Research in Norway*, 1974, pp. 8–17.

re Irish Voyaging

Chapman, Paul H., *The Man Who Led Columbus to America*. Atlanta: One Candle Press (Formerly Judson Press) 1973.

Dicuili, J. J. Tierney, *Dicuili Liber de Mensura Orbis Terrae*. Dublin: The Dublin Institute for Advanced Studies, 1967.

Selmer, Carl, *Navigatio Sancti Brendani Abbatis*. Notre Dame: University of Notre Dame Press, 1959.

Severin, Tim, *The Brendan Voyage*. New York: McGraw Hill, 1978.

re Multiple Voyaging

Cameron, Ian, *Lodestone and Evening Star*. New York: E. P. Dutton & Co., Inc., 1966.

Cumming, W., R. A. Shelton, and D. B. Quinn, *The Discovery of North America*. New York: American Heritage Press, 1972.

Lehner, Ernst and Johanna, *How They Saw the New World*. New York: Tudor Publishing Company, 1966.

Morison, Samuel Eliot, *The European Discovery of America*. New York: Oxford University Press, 1971.

Sauer, Carl O., *Northern Mists*, Berkely, CA: University of California Press, 1968.

re Columbus

Chapman, Paul H., *The Man Who Led Columbus to America.* Atlanta: One Candle Press (Formerly Judson Press) 1973.

Colon, Fernando, *The Life of the Admiral Christopher Columbus by His Son Ferdinand,* translated by Benjamin Keen, Rutgers University Press, New Brunswick, New Jersey, 1959.

Jane, Cecil, translator, *The Journal of Christopher Columbus.* New York: Bramhall House, 1960.

Landstrom, Bjorn, *Columbus.* New York: The Macmillan Company, 1966.

Las Casas, Bartolome de, *History of the Indies,* translated by Andree M. Collard, Harper and Rowe, New York, 1971.

Morison, Samuel Eliot, *Admiral of the Ocean Sea.* Boston: Little, Brown and Company, 1942. In paperback; *Christopher Columbus, Mariner.* Boston: Little, Brown and Company, 1942.

re Navigation

Bragger, A. W. and Haason Shetelig, *The Viking Ships.* Oslo: Dreyers Forlag, 1951 and 1971. English translation by Katherine John.

Mister, George W., *Primer of Navigation.* New York: Van Nostrand, 1940 and 1943.

re Other

Buchanan, Donal B., "The Spirit Pond Stones—Hoax or History?" *Popular Archaeology,* Vol. 4, Nos. 5–6, May–June, 1975.

Mallery, Arlington, *The Rediscovery of Lost America.* New York: Dutton, 1951 & 1979.

Sherwin, Reider T., *The Viking and the Red Man.* New York: Funk and Wagnalls, 1940.

Steffansson, Vilhjalmur, *Discovery.* New York: McGraw-Hill Book Co., 1964.

re Maps and Charts, Current

For elevations and ground topography: Sectional Charts. (small scale—1:500,000), World Aeronautical Charts. (medium scale—1:1,000,000), and Jet Navigation Charts. (large scale—1:2,000,000), National Oceanic and Atmospheric Administrations, Riverdale, MD 20840.

For nautical charts showing soundings, U.S. Nautical Charts, same address as above.

For nautical charts, Canada: Geoscience Maps, (small scale—1:300,000) (medium scale—1:1,000,000) (large scale—1:6,750,000). Canadian Hydrographic Services, Ottawa.

For nautical winds and currents: Pilot Charts of the North Atlantic Ocean, published for each month of the year by United States Naval Oceanographic Service, Washington.

Index

Kjartan, 65
Knattleikr, 90
Krossaness, 33, 46

L

Labrador, 16, 18, 21, 28, 33, 37, 39, 46, 50, 58, 60, 63, 65–67, 69, 76, 80, 87, 89–91, 102
LaCrosse, 90
Lake Melville, 46
Landnamabok, 6–7, 50, 62
Langaness, 50
L'Anse Aux Meadows, 1–2, 24, 60, 87, 91, 93
La Nuova Francia, 72
Larsen, Sophus, 102
Lee, Thomas E., 88
Leif's houses, 24, 28–29, 46, 52, 58, 60–61, 83, 87
Leigh, Reverend, 94
Locke, Don, 93
Long Island Sound, 2
Long Range Mountains, 29
Lysufjord, 36

M

Magdalen, 33
Magnusson, Magnus, 2, 57, 80
Maine, 28, 76, 83, 88
Maine State Museum, 88
Mallery, Arlington, 89–90
March, Mary, 93–94
Mare Oceanum, 67
Markland, 21, 37, 46, 50, 58, 60, 63–65, 67, 89–90, 101
Marshall, Ingeborg, 94
Marsson, Ari, 65
Mary March Museum, 93
Matthias, 66
Mediterranean, 14
Mercator, Gerald, 73, 76, 90
Mercer, Norman, 24
Micmacs, 58
mooring holes, 88
Morison, Samuel Eliot, 2
Mt. Mitchell, 16

N

Napoleon, 64, 66
Narragansett Bay, 69, 73, 90
National Geographic, 1–3
Natkusiak, 89
New Brunswick, 29
New Found Land, 69, 102
Newfoundland, 1, 11, 16, 18, 21, 24, 28–29, 31, 33, 36, 42, 46, 50, 54, 57–58, 60–61, 63, 65, 67, 69, 80, 83, 87, 89–91, 93, 102

Newport Neck, 76
Newport Tower, 73, 76, 88
Nonsbawsut, 93–94
Norfolk-Newport News, Va., 42
Norman Vilia, 69, 76
Norumbega, 72–73, 90
Norse penny, 88
Northern Cape, 33
Norway, 6, 8–9, 52, 54, 58, 63–65, 73, 76, 95, 102
Notre Dame Bay, 18
Nova Francia, 69
Nova Scotia, 1, 28–29, 42, 61, 69

O

Oddson, Bishop Gisle, 67
Orkney Islands, 64
Orteluis, Abraham, 72
Oslo, Norway, 6

P

Palsson, Herman, 80
Peyton, John, Jr., 93–94
Phoenicians, 64
Pining, Didrik, 102
Pistolet Bay, 21, 24, 29, 33, 46, 60, 83
Plymouth, Mass., 73, 76
Pohl, Fredrick J., 88
Poincy, De Quincit, 89
Polo, Marco, 102
Port au Port, 33
Port du Refuge, 72
Port Real, 72
Portolan Charts, 11, 14, 69
Portugal, 14, 102
Pothorst, 102
Prince Edward Island, 29, 33
Ptolemy, 99, 101

Q

Quebec, 31, 60, 76, 88, 90
Quebec City, 28

R

Ramskou, Thorkild, 9
Rasmusio, Giovanni, 69
Rea, Dr. John, 89
Red Indian Lake, 93
Resolution Island, 37
Reuben, Walter, 72
Reykjavik, 99
Rhineland foot, 76